MW01234878

Academic Conferences
for
Teachers and School Leaders

A K-12 Guide to Creating Collaboration for
Teachers, School, and District leaders

Eli R. Johnson & Arthur L. Costa

Achievement-4-All Publishers

Academic Conferences for Teachers and School Leaders

Achievement For All Publishers
Sacramento, CA 95682
(530) 391-1249
www.achievement4all.org

For information about permission to reproduce selections from this book please call (530) 391-1249 or go to www.achievement4all.org

Authors: Johnson, Eli R. & Costa, Arthur L.

Title: Academic Conferences for Teachers and School Leaders

Table of Contents

About the Authors

Foreword

About the Authors

Eli Johnson is a Classroom Teacher, School Principal, Director of Curriculum & Instruction, and Assistant Superintendent of Instruction. He has served as a consultant to the California Department of Education supporting early literacy, English language professional development, and math/science partnerships. He earned his teaching degree from Brigham Young University and education leadership degree from the University of Washington. In 2010, Eli led an elementary school to the highest annual gain (+140) of all the 10,000 schools in the state of California. He also directed a high school with 90% English Language Learners to become the recipient of the U.S. News and World Report Medal Award Honors. As a nationally recognized speaker and consultant, Eli works with teachers and leaders to support adolescent literacy, school leadership, and other issues affecting student achievement. Eli has worked for both public and non-profit educational organizations to create sustainable educational reform. You can contact Eli by e-mail at eli@achievement4all.org.

Art Costa is a Professor of Education, Emeritus, from California State University, Sacramento, where he taught graduate courses to teachers and administrators in curriculum, supervision, and the improvement of instruction. He is the author of *The Enabling Behaviors, Teaching for Intelligent Behaviors and Supervision for Intelligent Teaching*; and is co-author of *Cognitive Coaching and Techniques for Teaching Thinking*. He has written numerous other articles and publications on supervision, teaching strategies and thinking skills. Dr. Costa has made presentations and conducted workshops for educators throughout the United States and in Canada, Mexico, Europe, Africa, the Middle East, Asia and the South Pacific. He taught in the Bellflower School District, worked as a curriculum consultant in the Los Angeles County Superintendent of Schools Office, and was Assistant Superintendent of the Sacramento County Superintendent of Schools office. Active in many professional organizations, Dr. Costa has served as president of the California Association for Supervision and Curriculum Development and as president of the national A.S.C.D. from 1988 to 1989. Art can be reached by e-mail at artcosta@aol.com

Acknowledgements

We would like to thank all of those who reviewed, revised, and gave valuable feedback throughout the developmental process of designing academic conferences. Doug Mills is a genius with crafting the right words to highlight important ideas. Scott Rungwerth implemented the conferral processes in the high school setting and provided tremendous insights. Appreciation goes to Steve Marks, Jr. who gave his support and energy to the conferencing framework. Linda Rungwerth used her experience in elementary schools to outline many of the key formatting for the academic conference template. And, most of all we would like to thank our wonderful wives who have encouraged us over the years to focus on the processes for developing collaboration and collegiality in our schools.

Other Books

Published by

Achievement-4-All

Achievement-4-All Publishers

Foreword

We currently face exciting times in education. While the challenges our students confront each day seem to increase, our knowledge and understanding of what works in schools is also increasing. Over the years, schools have added common core standards, comprehensive curriculum, instructional strategies, academic assessments, and educational collaboration to meet the needs of all our students. Collaborating together as educational professionals has enhanced our educational results. As teacher leaders, school leaders, and district leaders we can improve academic outcomes through innovations in educational collaboration. As we work together, we can create results through a growing educational movement called academic conferences.

Like professional learning communities, academic conferences increase collaboration and support collegial dialogue. Academic conferencing between teachers, principals, and district administrators provide us a forum as professionals to consider our educational practices and plan for future results. Conferencing provides opportunities to explore new outcomes for the school organization. In our roles as instructional leaders (whether as a teacher, site administrator, or district administrator), it seems we rarely take the time to conference together and address the most important academic challenges we face. Academic conferral sessions are designed to help educators identify how teaching tasks and academic outcomes in the classroom connect to the long-term strategic plans, learning goals, and academic purposes of the district. This book is about encouraging and enhancing these conferral conversations. A quick story illustrates how academic conferences can influence some of our common challenges.

> *. . . We had just started new roles within a struggling school district — Eli as Chief Academic Officer in the central office and Art as leadership consultant for the district. We helped implement academic conferences within the schools and conducted academic conferences at the district level. When we started conducting academic conferences our academic initiatives really took hold and took off. When teachers conferred with school leadership teams and principals conferred with district leadership teams, everyone's ideas and efforts were brought together to produce consistent results. As the year progressed, the teachers and principals embraced both the opportunity to openly discuss their important ideas and the chance to work together. As we look back, we have often reflected on the impact of academic conferences and marveled at how these collegial conversations made such a difference. . .*

Conferencing allows teachers, principals, and district administrators to take the time to look at instructional practice in depth. When done effectively, academic conferences can transform our schools and help school and teacher leaders achieve excellence in every classroom for every student. Let's take a look at what we will be discussing and discovering in the upcoming chapters:

Chapter 1: Academic Conferences for Teachers and School Leaders

This chapter highlights the importance of academic conferences in focusing teacher and school leaders on student learning and instructional leadership. We will look at an overview of both classroom-teacher conferences and school-administrator conferences and discover how they help create vertical alignment within our schools and school districts.

Chapter Two: Academic Conferences for Classroom-Teachers

This chapter provides an overview of the role academic conferences play in transforming our schools. The roles of facilitator, supporters, and chief contributor are outlined. The who, what, where, when, and why of these academic conferences are discussed. We look at an overview of academic conferences and how they can improve the academic results in our classrooms.

Chapter Three: Key Principles of Classroom-Teacher Academic Conferences

This chapter identifies the conferral feedback processes that create effective school-wide conferences. The five conferral processes of reflecting on instruction, analyzing student data, planning and setting goals, creating solutions, and making commitments will be emphasized. An academic conference template is provided that provides a road map for conducting effective conferences.

Chapter Four: How to Conduct Classroom-Teacher Conferences

We will look at the in's and out's of conducting classroom-teacher conferences. This chapter discusses how to engage in classroom-teacher academic conferences so that personal trust develops and academic performance improves. Specific examples of dialogue and "how to do it" insights are provided.

Chapter Five: Academic Conferences for School-Administrators

Chapter five highlights the roles for school-administrator conferences. We will look at developing a common vision through academic conferences. The specific skills for chief contributors (principals and their admin team), facilitators (assistant superintendent or other district administrator), supporters (directors of instruction, special education, ELL, etc.) are addressed. We will note the need for an organizational change in education by conducting school-administrator conferences.

Chapter Six: Key Principles of School-Administrator Academic Conferences

This chapter identifies key principles for creating learning organizations through effective school-administrator conferences. The conferral process of reflecting, analyzing data, planning, creating solutions, and making commitments for school administrators is addressed.

Chapter Seven: How to Conduct School-Administrator Academic Conferences

This chapter identifies the how-to's for implementing effective school-administrator conferences. Creating a shared vision through conferencing is outlined. Specific examples of administrative conversations and "how to do it" insights are provided.

Chapter Eight: Leading and Sustaining Academic Conferences

This chapter addresses the need creating self-directed learning, ownership and interdependent trust between classroom and school leaders. Implementation, capacity building, and sustainability for academic conferences are covered. We will outline methods for school-wide and district-wide certification for staff members. We will review the key principles that make academic conferences innovative and successful.

Academic conferences are intentional interactions that place learning at the center of the conversation. Educational leaders should engage their colleagues in these structured discussions several times throughout the school year. Academic conferences are like a new ray of sunshine for collegiality and collaboration between instructional leaders. We hope you enjoy learning about these educational conferral processes for improving academic outcomes and results.

Chapter One:

Academic Conferences for Teachers and School Leaders

"To listen closely and reply well
is the highest perfection
we are able to attain
in the art of conversation."

François de La Rochefoucauld

Albert adjusted his tie for the sixth time. Ties made him uncomfortable. They felt more like a noose than an accessory. He shuffled his notes one last time as he braced himself to stand before his academic colleagues. He preferred the privacy of his research--instead he was about to present his latest work before his professional peers. This was not the first time he had been asked to speak in front of a large group, but he keenly felt the magnitude of such a gathering of great minds. His most recent ideas and perspectives were gaining steam and he worried how they might be received. He'd spent the last hour anticipating the challenging questions he'd be asked in the follow up. In some ways, it would be the hardest part. Albert knew the reaction to this presentation had the potential to shape the future of his life's work.

Marie's hands were shaking ever so slightly. She felt both excited and nervous at the same time. As the first female professor at the distinguished Sorbonne in France she had come far. But the need to prove her never ceased. Even though she had already received the Nobel Prize in Chemistry, she knew her work was about to be subjected to careful attention. This was a special treat, since the best and brightest were gathered to advance the profession. It felt like both a privilege and a pleasure to rub shoulders with her academic peers. She had enjoyed the other presentations and now it was her turn.

Ernest sank into his chair while he listened to his colleague's present one genius idea after another. The pressure was off now that his presentation was done. He was satisfied with how the conference had come along. The intellectual dialogue with other experts in his profession had been engrossing, to the point that Ernest had lost track of time. As one of the more experienced members of the group, he had thoroughly enjoyed their time together, joking with old friends and encouraging the fresh newcomers to the field. He truly felt the insights and concepts generated from this conference would transform his work. He'd even been inspired to make changes in his approach to his research. His professional pursuits were now richer and even more rewarding than ever before.

These vignettes take a peek into the lives of three of the most famous scientists of the previous century--Albert Einstein, Marie Curie, and Ernest Rutherford. Each of them received the Nobel Prize for their discoveries related to the atom. Einstein shared his theory of relativity and the famous $E = MC^2$. Curie discovered the elements "polonium" and "radium." Rutherford developed a concept for quantum mechanics. Their discoveries still impact our world today. All three joined their colleagues at the Academic Conference in Solvay, Belgium held in 1911. Many of the greatest scientists of the last century sat in the same room, discussing the issues surrounding their personal work and the developing their profession of scientific research. The time spent questioning and conferring with other experts in their field stimulated self-discovery and self-directed learning. This Academic Conference developed interdependence between scientists all over the world. Scientists from completely different areas of research were now challenging each other and creating a collegiality that led to new discoveries.

Figure 1.1: *The Solvay Academic Conference held in 1911. Einstein (standing 2nd from right), Curie (sitting 2nd from right), Rutherford (standing 3rd from right next to Einstein), and 26 other participants became Nobel Prize Winners.*

Innovative Progress

The Solvay Science Academic Conference and subsequent conferences became pivotal points in the success of the science profession. The profession of scientific research experienced unprecedented progress in the last century. The collaboration created through academic conferences energized the field. Scientists no longer worked in isolation. The academic conferences propelled new discoveries and refined various theories as they developed. They definitely made a difference. These professional conferences provided the vehicle that would see dramatic improvements in the science profession over the next century. Because of the collegial conferencing, science and medicine emerged from secluded labs and back rooms into a shared environment where ideas were openly exchanged and innovative insights were given the light of day. The scientist was no longer a "one-man" show. The field of science had become a *learning community of scientists*. The discoveries revealed at every Academic Conference impacted the next few years, which in turn impacted new discoveries. They provided a structure by which a self-perpetuating cycle of discovery built upon itself continually. This practice has continued to shape history for the last hundred years. Scientific research is now one of the most influential professions in the world, affecting the global economy and the way people relate to each other and the world around them.

Creating Academic Focus

While science, medicine, and other professions have conferred at academic conferences to improve their profession, in education we still have a ways to go. Our profession as educators in many ways is at a crossroads. As we strive to generate solutions to our collective challenges, we need to find ways to work together towards a shared vision. Aligning everyone together around a shared vision takes both time and understanding. A clear pathway can only be developed as we work together as true professionals and develop a unity of purpose. As instructional leaders, we need to work together to strengthen the foundation of education as a professional field. The overarching vision of our school systems should focus and confer on two top priorities (Pashler, 2007):

❖ **Student Learning** for all students
❖ **Instructional Leadership** in every classroom

Our school systems need to operate in ways that support learning and increases our abilities as instructional leaders. When do we ever really take the time to discuss the important priorities of student learning instructional leadership? As we consider these two primary purposes of our schools-- *student learning and instructional leadership*--we recognize them as the important priorities of our schools, yet it seems we rarely take the time to make sure that they are working effectively. It is important that the key individuals in the instructional process (teacher, principals, and district administrator) take the time to discuss student learning and instructional leadership in our schools.

The Missing Piece in our Schools

Today we have a research base as well as assessment tools in education to make professional decisions. Some conversations happen in the parking lot or out on the black-top, yet professional conversations in education almost never happen between the instructional leaders of the school—teachers and principals. We need an environment where we can sit down together and talk pointedly and specifically about our educational vision and the direction we are taking. As professional organizations, our schools need to address the key issues that affect our students, teachers, and administrators. Education is in many ways a local and personal practice, and we need to develop solutions that will improve student learning

Figure 1.2: *Academic Conferences provide the missing piece we need to unite all teacher, school and district leaders around student learning and instruction.*

Real conversations about instruction, amongst the leaders of our classrooms and schools, seem to happen all too infrequently. We need to have continuing, open conversations about the crucial instructional issues that we face in our classrooms and in our schools.

Academic Conferences

Academic conferences provide a systematic and consistent method for each of us to examine our professional practice and personal progress. Whether we call them *"Academic Conferences"*, *"Educational Summits"*, *"Data Dialogues"* or *"Instructional Conversations"*, these conferencing sessions provide a forum for focusing our school conversations firmly on student results. These discussions must be deliberate and intentional; the key is to focus the dialogue on student learning and instructional leadership. Academic Conferences are essential to developing our profession. They provide us with the time we need to plan proactively for improvement. They provide the vehicle for exploring research-based strategies, identifying innovative ideas, and incorporating proven practices in our schools. Academic Conferences, at their core, are collegial conversations that take place between instructional leaders (teachers with school administrators and school administrators with district administrators) to improve student results.

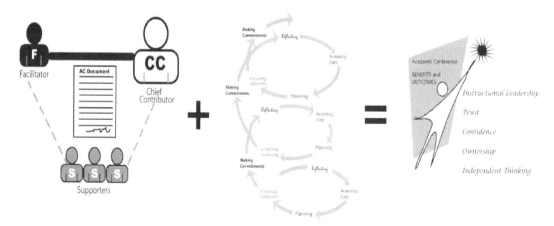

Figure 1.3: *The Academic Conference Model provides roles and relationships, conferral process cycle, and powerful benefits.*

In a time and era when district-wide initiatives like Response to Intervention (RTI) are enhancing our profession, we need to carve out time to meet and really discuss and coordinate our efforts towards student progress (Johnson & Karns, 2011). The primary purpose of this time is to confer together as colleagues about the academic progress and needs of our students. Academic Conferences are the missing piece to our schools achieving consistent results. Addressing academic concerns in student achievement takes a cohesive and coordinated effort. Wellman & Lipton (2001) point out that:

> *"When we accept the notion that the way we currently respond to student learning needs produces current results, we come to realize that if we want different results we will have to learn to respond differently. These responses will need to occur at both the instructional and organizational level if we want more students to reach greater and deeper levels of learning."*

Let's now talk about two different types of academic conferences within our school organizations.

Two Types of Academic Conferences in Education

We not only need to create horizontal professional community where this can happen between teachers, but we also need to create vertical professional communities between teachers and site administrators and site administrators and district administrators.

- ❖ **Classroom-Teacher Academic Conferences**
- ❖ **School-Administrator Academic Conferences**

A variety of school meetings happen throughout the year, but the vast majority of them have little to do with improving instruction and supporting the work of teachers and students in the classroom. Academic conferences organize and increase instructional leadership among teachers, principals, and district administrators.

Classroom-Teacher Academic Conferences

In education, we say that we strongly believe in things like instructional leadership and collaboration. Yet it seems we rarely get together as administrative and classroom leaders to discuss the issues that directly affect our classrooms and our students. Classroom-Teaching Academic Conferences are designed for supporting instruction, student learning, and classroom teachers.

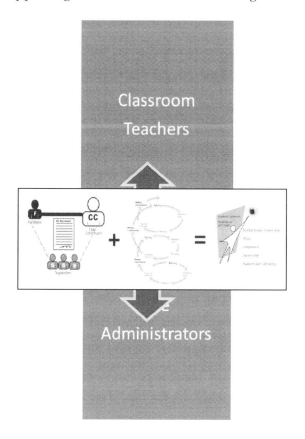

Figure 1.4: *Classroom-Teacher Academic Conferences provide vertical alignment between classroom teachers and school administrators*

As we open up our private practice and pursue common professional purposes, we will see positive success for our students. They are typically facilitated by school administrators. They address the needs of individual students and focus everyone's combined efforts on student learning. Let's take a look at how

School-Administrator Academic Conferences

School

The research reveals to no surprise that the classroom teacher has the greatest impact on student success and school principals have the second greatest impact (Marzano et al., 2001). At the same time, teachers consistently benefit from a process of identifying educational needs, clarifying instructional plans, sharing proven practices, and tracking student progress (Picciano, 2006). It feels obvious, and in a lot of ways, it is. But, there is a lack of current structure in our schools for this truly to take place as a planned initiative that specifically supports students, teachers, and administrator success. Now let's consider the other academic conference that will vertically align instruction within our school organizations. School-Administrating Academic Conferences are designed to support school principals and their leadership teams. They are typically led by the District Superintendent or Assistant Superintendent of Instruction. They address the strategic vision for each school and the major initiatives of the district. Through the conferral process the instructional vision for the district becomes a shared vision. They ensure that everyone keeps their collective "eye on the prize" for students. Schein (2004) points out that,

"Much has been said of the need for vision in leaders, but too little has been said of their need to listen, to absorb, to search the environment for trends, and to build the organization's capacity to learn."

These conferences also help develop leadership within each individual in the organization, and in turn, the entire organization itself. We need to be explicit about our goals for our students and clearly outline and conference about the steps that it will take to ensure they achieve these learning goals. We also need to be explicit about the goals for our schools and clearly identify the instructional initiatives that will increase school-wide results. School-administrator conferences focus our collective efforts on the vision of the district and on the learning of our students. As we take the time and devote our energies to coordinating our academic plans, then we will be able to work together to achieve instructional results.

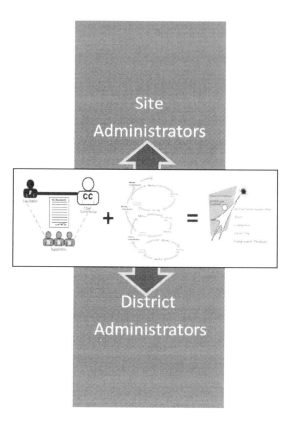

Figure 1.5: *School-Administrator Academic Conferences align the efforts of the school and district.*

Academic conferences are intentional interactions that place learning at the center of the conversation. Educational leaders should engage their colleagues in these structured discussions several times throughout the school year. Conducting classroom-teacher and school-administrator conferences actively supports success for our students and schools. We will discuss School-Administrators Academic Conferences in greater detail in Chapters 4 and Chapters 5.

Current Collaborative Efforts

A current movement in education that has positively impacted the profession of education is Professional Learning Communities (DuFour et al., 2009). Professional Learning Communities or (PLC's) have carved out time for teachers to meet as professionals to discuss common classroom concerns. PLC's have aligned teachers horizontally (i.e. grade level, subject matter, etc.) with their peers. Our schools benefit from these horizontal discussions amongst teachers as we talk with other grade level peers about our subject matter.

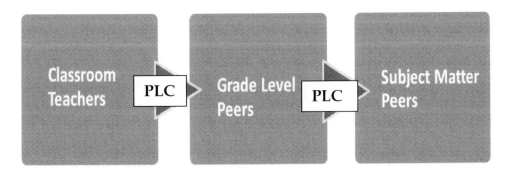

Figure1.6: *Professional Learning Communities help horizontally align school organizations*

Professional Learning Communities (PLC's) align teachers with other teachers horizontally, yet we also need to align the purposes of educators with one another vertically. Academic conferences provide a new movement in educational collaboration by connecting educators within the school organization vertically.

Vertically Aligning Instructional Leadership

Academic conferences align instructional leadership throughout the entire organization. They provide positive support for teachers (classroom leaders) at the school level, as well as support for principals (school leaders) at the district level.

Vertical Alignment within School-Administrator Conferences

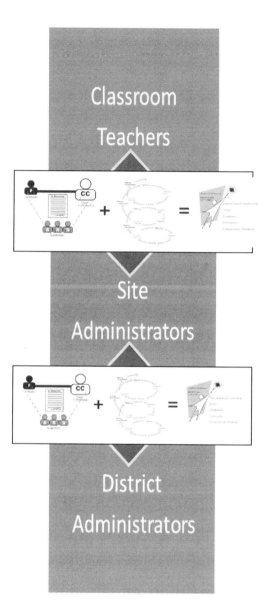

Figure 1.7: *Classroom-teacher academic conferences align instructional purposes within our classrooms, and school-administrator academic conferences help align instructional purposes within our schools.*

Academic conferences are designed for educational professionals to coordinate and communicate academic progress about our schools and classrooms. Academic conferences vertically align the efforts of the entire school organization. When classroom-teacher conferences and school-administrator conferences are conducted consistently throughout the district organization, then the academic vision of the district has a much better chances of being successfully implemented. While professional learning communities or PLCs help create horizontal alignment between teachers in common grade levels and content areas, academic conferences help create vertical alignment between the efforts of teachers, principals, and district leaders. We can also view academic conferences as opportunities to link classroom teachers to site administrators, and in turn link site administrators to district administrators.

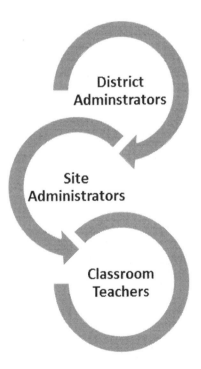

Figure 1.8: Academic conferences help district administrators to work with site administrators and in turn these school principals are better able to support classroom teachers to achieve the academic vision for all students.

Summary

In these ever-changing times, it is even more essential in the profession of education that we engage in academic conferences to ensure the collective efforts of individual educators will successfully contribute to the core mission, goals, values, and instructional vision of the school organization. Conferring aligns the efforts of classroom teachers and school principals with the mission, initiatives, and vision surrounding student learning and improving instruction. In many ways academic conferences achieve greater results, since they have the ability to align and integrate all of these educational movements into the culture and core fabric of the school system. Conferencing encourages us to plan and reflect on our professional practices and organizational progress. Just as professional learning communities (PLCs) have supported teachers with horizontal collaboration, academic conferences strengthen both classroom teachers and school administrators with vertical support. They provide a reflective examination of the school's collective progress, as well as each individual's own purposes, practices, and progress to achieve the collective educational mission. Conferring together supports interdependent leadership where every educator plays a valuable role in working together to create solutions for kids. The ultimate benefit of academic conferences is more student learning and increased quality instruction. As we embrace the opportunity to work collegially as a team and align our common purposes in our profession, then our students will benefit the most.

Reflection Questions:

1. *How can Academic Conferences help your school organization and develop instructional leadership within the members of your organization?*

2. *What are the potential benefits for implementing Academic Conferences in your school and district?*

Chapter Two:

Academic Conferences for

Classroom-Teachers

*"To listen closely and reply well is the highest perfection
we are able to attain in the art of conversation."*

François de La Rochefoucauld

Ms. Adams looked around her classroom and organized some last minute lesson plans for the sub. Her mind was racing about the academic conference she was about to have. She said goodbye to the sub and walked past trees turning to reds and yellows. She wondered, "Why do I get to be the first one to share with the principal how my students are doing?" It seemed having the last name Adams meant alphabetically she was first up once again. As the first teacher to go through an academic conference at her school, she felt like a guinea pig. But, first for what? She figured she'd find out soon enough. Her fellow teachers reminded her repeatedly that she had to report back to them all of the sordid details. She braced herself as she walked into the conference room; the principal, assistant principal, counselor, and the instructional coach all met her with a smile. She wondered if they were really happy to see her, or if they were smiling because they were going to feed her to the lions for having "problem students". She knew that several of her students were having academic difficulties but would the conference really make a positive difference? . . . Thirty-five minutes later Ms. Adams left amazed by what had just happened. She thought, "The other teachers aren't going to believe me."

Transforming Instructional Support

Our classrooms and schools need to experience a dramatic turnaround. This change in education must be much more than just "school reformation". It needs to be a school *transformation*. If we want to transform our schools, we need to focus on improving the *internal* processes. Transformation only happens from the inside out. A transformation must affect the internal processes of the education system that often get overlooked. Academic conferences benefit our struggling schools by providing educational interactions that can transform how teachers are supported in their work. The conferences serve as a forum for counteracting the challenges of disconnected teachers and schools. Classroom teachers and school principals have the ability to collectively transform our schools. We must begin changing our schools from isolated, segregated, and unconnected experiences to transparent, trusting, and united learning environments that truly transform how we work with students and with each other. We have "reformed" so many things in education from the school calendars, the bussing routes, cafeteria menus, daily schedules, and an endless list of other external factors. The problem is just that: they are all *external* factors. Transforming our schools is not a singular event that happens with the wave of a magic wand. It is a focused set of processes that continuously work towards and achieve academic progress. This transformational process incorporates a series of academic conference sessions that cohesively hold together the actions, accountability, and achievement of the individuals involved. To improve our profession Price Waterhouse Coopers (2001) note that,

> *"An essential strand will be to reduce teacher workload, foster increased teacher ownership, and create the capacity to manage change in a sustainable way that can lay the foundation for improved school and pupil performance in the future."*

Academic conferences offer a solution that requires each participant to *participate*, to take ownership of the challenges of their students and their school and to take the responsibility for creating and maintaining real solutions to these problems. The academic conference provides the framework where true ownership can happen.

Supporting Teacher Contributions

It seems that teachers rarely receive the attention and support they deserve. And the sixty four thousand dollar question is: *when do teachers and principals ever talk about the real issues that face our students?* The classroom-teacher academic conference brings the teacher and principal together with support staff to confer about the issues that face our students. The list of challenges that teachers experience seems to grow by the day. Studies have shown that teaching is the second most stressful profession (Jarvis, 2003). Our schools need to target teacher stressors and develop sustainable solutions for our profession. Sarason (1990) points out that,

> *"...when a process makes people feel that they have a voice in matters that affect them, they will have great commitment to the overall enterprise and will take greater responsibility for what happens to the enterprise."*

He also notes that research identifies several academic challenges that face our teachers that we should take efforts to :

As teachers we often feel isolated. Teachers rarely have a chance to engage in conversations regarding important instructional decisions. New teachers are often left to their own devices, and it results in a high number of new teachers abandoning the profession. Academic conferences provide teachers and administrators the time to meet, reflect, plan, and talk with each other. Instruction and learning are dynamic processes that are influenced by the challenges that students bring with them to school.

As teachers we often lack a sense of influence and empowerment. Teachers are the most important factor in the improvement of student learning—yet they are usually the last ones to be consulted about decisions concerning curriculum, professional development, instructional practices, interventions, and assessment procedures.

As teachers we often receive little effective support. Rather than use observations and quantitative data to consistently inform instruction, teachers receive rare evaluations that have a coercive tone. The feedback rarely provides teachers the opportunity to reflect on, review, and improve their instructional practices.

Without allocating time for frequent conferencing, the teaching profession tends to be viewed as a fragmented and isolated experience. Both experienced and new teachers alike can sometimes feel lost or alone in meeting the growing demands of achievement for all students (Johnson & Karns, 2011). One can only believe that there has got to be a better way.

Transforming Instructional Culture

Academic conferences are the catalyst for transforming school and classroom culture, because they provide the mechanisms for shifting the organization to greater achievements. The more time that academic conferences are integrated into the learning culture of the school then the more a feedback spiral of understanding will produce ever increasing results. Studies by Karen Seashore Louis and colleagues (1996) have identified five areas that characterize a vibrant academic culture in successful schools:

1) **Reflective Dialogue**. Reflective practice implies self-awareness about one's work as a teacher. By engaging in in-depth conversations about teaching and learning, teachers can examine their instructional practice.

2) **A Collective Focus on Student Learning**. An undeviating concentration on student learning is a core characteristic of school communities

3) **Shared Expectations and Values.** There is a sense of common values and expectations among members of a school community.

4) **Professional Collaboration.** Collaborative work with administrators and teachers increases everyone's affiliation with one other and the school.

5) Transparent Instructional Practice. In professional communities, teachers reflect and share their classroom practices.

Effective schools and districts achieve these outcomes throughout the school culture by engaging in dialogue that allows for sharing of expectations, time for collaborative conferencing, and time for reflection on instructional practices.

Learning Conversations and Classroom-Teacher Academic Conferences

At the heart of successful schools are authentic learning conversations that create effective learning organizations. These learning conversations should be focused on the twin purposes of student learning and the quality instruction that supports student learning. Academic conferences provide the time, space, and capacity to conduct learning conversations that benefit students. Looking at individual student data contributes to the quality of the learning conversations regarding student progress. Effective learning conversations need several key structures in order to be successful. Learning conversations allow the vision of learning organizations to inculcate effectively throughout the entire school system. Leithwood & Poplin (1992) point out that,

> *"One of our studies suggests that teacher motivation for development is enhanced when they adopt a set of internalized goals for professional growth. School leaders can do their part by helping to ensure that such goals are clear, explicit, and ambitious enough to be challenging and realistic. Feedback from colleagues about discrepancies between their goals for growth and their current practices can be especially helpful."*

Academic conversations are purposeful conversations that reveal instructional intent. They are designed to achieve specific academic outcomes like reflecting, planning, creating solutions, and committing. Effective learning organizations outline the roles of learning and provide time for individuals to discuss the progress in their respective roles.

Classroom-Teacher Academic Conferences Create Support

Academic conferences bring teachers, principals, and support professionals to the table to discuss the most important focus for our schools: student learning and classroom instruction. The following diagram shows the three key roles for organizing academic conferences:

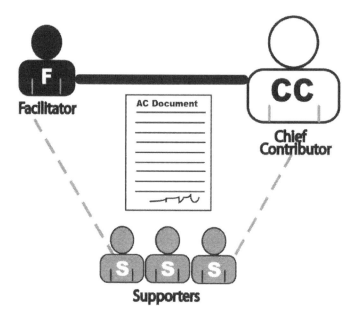

Figure 2.1: *Academic Conference Roles and Relationships work to create collaboration*

Academic conferences provide a clear focus for classroom teachers and site leaders to meet and discuss the academic progress of schools and students. Aligning the vision, interests, and actions of everyone at the school site allows the school to move forward effectively and efficiently.

Vertical Alignment within School Organizations

School-administrator academic conferences connect the vision and leadership of the district with the leadership and implementation of school administrators. Without each individual stepping into their role as an academic leader, the school will be unable to move in a strong direction as a unified body.

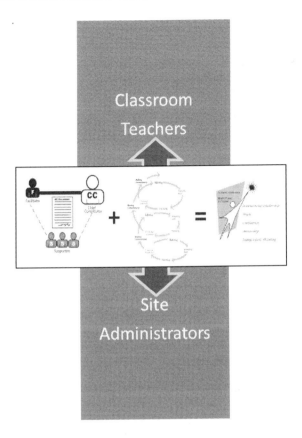

Figure 2.2: *Classroom-Teacher Conferences Align learning efforts between teachers and school administrators.*

Creating an environment and culture where key instructional leaders (teachers and principals) can dialogue and discuss reflective feedback together is important for academic progress. Isolation, lack of influence, and limited feedback all contribute to feeling our efforts are increasingly distant and impersonal, so it is important that we work together to align our collective efforts through classroom-teacher academic conferences.

Roles and Relationships

The roles established in academic conferences are designed to enlist the best thinking of everyone at the table. We have the ability to create solutions to the challenges that face our students. The relationships in academic conferences need to be made safe by encouraging open dialogue and frank discussion of student data results and their specific needs. There are three main roles at the academic conference:

- ❖ **Chief Contributor** (classroom teacher)
- ❖ **Facilitator** (typically the school principal)
- ❖ **Supporters** (assistant principal, counselor, academic coach, etc.)

The most important aspect of the academic conference is to strengthen the relationships of those who have responsibility for student learning. Our roles overlap and we have a collective ownership to work as interdependent leaders in behalf of our students.

We live in a day when isolated efforts will most often fall short of meeting the learning demands of our students. Developing these relationships in ways they can flourish takes a different approach than most typically considered. Let's take a quick look at each of the three roles outlined in academic conferences—facilitator, chief contributor, and supporters. We will take a more in depth look at the specific responsibilities of these roles as we talk about them in the upcoming chapters on Classroom-Teaching and School-Administrating Academic Conferences.

Facilitator's Role

The facilitator sets the stage for the academic conferences and helps lead the chief contributor to a successful conferral session. As a facilitator their role is to nudge and guide the conferral conversations forward (Costa & Garmston, 2002). The facilitator asks the focus question that helps keep the conversation on students and classroom learning. The facilitator also helps focus on classroom data and individual student data to determine successes and identify additional areas for instructional support. As they effectively interact with the chief contributor they can help bring innovative thinking and creative solutions to the surface. The facilitator is usually the school principal, yet any school support staff who is trained can effectively facilitate classroom-teacher conference sessions.

Facilitator

Figure 2.3: *The school principal primarily serves as the facilitator in classroom-teacher academic conferences.*

The facilitator creates an atmosphere of trust where ideas can be shared, instructional plans can be made, student data can be analyzed, solutions can be developed, and commitments are made. There are five skills that are essential to facilitating effective academic conferences.

Facilitator Key Skills

- ❖ *Asking Focus Questions*
- ❖ *Analyzing Classroom Data*
- ❖ *Encouraging Plans and Goals*
- ❖ *Suggesting Solutions*
- ❖ *Confirming Commitments*

Typically the principal assumes the facilitator role at the classroom-teacher academic conference, yet anyone who is trained in the key processes of facilitating can fulfill this role. The facilitator (principal) begins the academic conference by asking a focus question that helps guide the dialogue of the conferral session. The facilitator also provides classroom and student data on a projector so that everyone in the room can visibly see and analyze the data. Patterns and trends are identified and the chief contributor (teacher) then identifies five students that they will focus on over the next eight weeks to see if they can significantly make academic progress with these specific students. Once the data has been viewed and five students have been targeted, the facilitator helps the chief contributor establish plans and set three goals that the teacher will work on for the next eight weeks to increase learning outcomes for all students. If the teacher feels she needs help creating a solution to a challenge in the classroom, the facilitator can offer three suggestions that may help student learning. Finally, the facilitator will identify one professional growth area the teacher would like to work on and then confirm the three commitments made by the teacher and in turn make one commitment back to the teacher to support instruction and learning in the classroom.

A Variety of Individuals may serve as the Facilitator

The principal will most often serve as the primary facilitator for classroom academic conferences. Yet, the assistant principal, academic coach, counselor, department chair, or other team member can serve as the facilitator for the conference. For large high schools with over 70-80 teachers, responsibilities for conducting academic conferences may need to be shared and other members will need to regularly take on the facilitator responsibilities. Schein (2004) notes that:

> *"A paradox of learning leadership is that the leader must be able not only to lead but also to listen, to involve the group in achieving its own insights into its cultural dilemmas, and to be genuinely participative in his or her approach to learning and change."*

When listening intently is used in an academic conference, greater relational trust can be developed between everyone throughout the organization. In-depth listening supports understanding during the academic conference, and it also creates an accumulated benefit as relational trust increases over time between individuals.

Chief Contributor's Role

The chief contributor is the primary individual who influences the academic conference. As we consider the challenges of students in the classroom, we know that the teacher is the most important individual to the success of the classroom. The ultimate success of the academic conference hinges on the chief contributor gathering the understanding that is gained, solutions that are created, and commitments that are made and then taking the actions to improve academic progress.

Figure 2.4: *The Chief Contributor is the Teacher and it is their expertise and ideas that drive the results of classroom-teacher academic conferences.*

The chief contributor is the most important individual at the academic conference, because they know the most about what is going on in their primary area of responsibility—the classroom or the school. In addition, the skills of reflection, analysis, planning, solution creating, and committing to purposeful action are the key processes that make academic conferences so powerful in achieving results for kids.

Chief Contributor Key Skills

- ❖ *Reflect on Instruction*
- ❖ *Analyze Student Data*
- ❖ *Plan and Set Goals*
- ❖ *Create Solutions*
- ❖ *Make Commitments*

The teacher is the chief contributor in the classroom-teaching conference, and the principal is the chief contributor in the school-administrating academic conference.

The chief contributor engages in dialogue and discussion with the facilitator in order to reflect on instruction, analyze student data and select five specific students to track progress, develop plans and set three goals, create classroom solutions, and choose one key professional development growth area The process of reflecting on instruction, analyzing data, selecting five students, setting three goals, and choosing one key professional growth area for the next eight weeks are powerful steps for improving instruction and student learning.

Supporter's Role

Supporters play a support role in the academic conference. The most important role the supporters play is to listen to the chief contributor so that they can understand additional ways to support the chief contributor. Supporters help with preparing data for the conference discussions and ensuring effective follow-through after the completion of the conferral sessions.

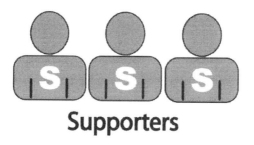

Supporters

Figure 2.5: *Supporters in Classroom-Teacher Conferences are typically assistant principals, school counselors, instructional coaches, etc.*

Supporters may take notes as needed to record the plans, solutions, and commitments made during the conference sessions. While supporters play a quiet, yet important role in the academic conference, their most lasting impact typically occurs through the actions they take to support their colleagues after the conference session. Supporters will learn a lot by being present at academic conferences.

Supporters Key Skills

- ❖ *Record Information*
- ❖ *Listen Intently*
- ❖ *Provide Follow-up Support*

In the Classroom-Teaching Academic Conferences the key supporters are usually instructional coaches, school counselors, resource specialists, and any other staff members who support instruction. The supporter's role in the conference is to listen and learn how they can better support individual teachers in the classroom and individual schools in the areas where they need it most. Supporters really provide their support by the actions they take after the conference session is over. They should take the information they glean and use it to provide targeted support in areas that support teacher instruction and student learning. Supporters play an important role of preserving a written record of ideas shared, plans made, and commitments to follow through on.

<u>Who</u> are the Major Players in Classroom-Teacher Conferences?

The academic conference pulls together the major players and puts them in one room with the responsibility of talking specifically about student learning.

Classroom Teacher – The classroom teacher is the most important person in the academic conference, and they serve as the **chief contributor**. They provide direction to the conference to meet the needs of their students. The teacher should bring information or evidence of student work that demonstrates individual student progress.

School Principal – The school principal typically serves as the **facilitator** for the classroom-teacher academic conference, and they are instructional leaders primarily responsible for keeping the dialogue and discussion focused on student needs and their learning progress.

Assistant Principal – The assistant principal(s) should also play an active role as a co-facilitator in the Academic Conference. At large schools with many teachers, assistant principals can be assigned to serves as the chief facilitator of the academic conferences.

Instructional Coaches or Department Chairs – Coaches can help interpret student data, reinforce ideas, and ask questions as co-facilitators of the conference. They can be assigned to take notes and record the needs of the teacher and individual students. The instructional Coach can use this valuable information to then support the teacher and students in the classroom during the upcoming weeks.

School Counselor or other Support Staff – Counselors and others may benefit from hearing specific feedback from teachers about how individual students are doing and what may be areas of need. They can prepare student data, run the LCD projector, or showcase student work.

Students represented by data – Ultimately students are the primary focal point of academic conferences. While they are not physically present at the conference, they are represented by data, classroom work, and vital information showcasing their academic performance and progress.

Conferencing is for anyone who wants to be part of creating a classroom, school, or district organization that works together for the benefit of all students, and for everyone who has the faith and belief to create such a place of learning.

What processes are covered in Classroom-Teacher Conferences?

Classroom-teacher Academic Conferences should primarily focus on the two primary purposes of school—student learning and quality instruction. The academic conference is a time to emphasize and dig deep into what the school values. The questions that the principal asks will guide the direction of the conversation and keep the dialogue and discussion flowing. The Academic Conference is a time of discovery where the instructional leaders share and discuss with one another academic progress in the classroom.

Conferral Processes that are covered include:

❖ **Reflect on Instructional Practice**
❖ **Analyze Student Data**
❖ **Plan and Set Goals**
❖ **Create Effective Solutions**
❖ **Make Academic Commitments**

When the five conferral processes are coordinated together, the classroom-teacher conferences create metacognitive reflection, understanding through data discussions, clear goals and plans, effective classroom solutions, and a commitment to work together to continually improve instruction and academic outcomes.

<u>Where</u> is the best place to hold Classroom-Teacher Conferences?

The Academic Conference should be held in a location where there will be no disruptions and the leadership team and teachers can interact comfortably. The library conference room, office conference room, or any other rooms where everyone can talk openly can work well. Sitting at a round or rectangle table where everyone see each other is important. The conference should have space for a projector where up-to-date student data can be displayed for everyone to review.

❖ **A quiet comfortable setting away from distractions**
❖ **A space where everyone (leadership team and teacher) can be at the table**
❖ **A space where a projector can display individual student data**

The Classroom-teacher academic conference should provide the space and time for instructional leaders (teacher, principal, coaches, etc.) to look at the data and discuss student's needs.

When should Classroom-Teacher Conferences be held?

Classroom-teacher Academic Conferences are typically held four times a year to support classroom-teachers, yet they can be held as frequently as needed. The first academic conference for each school year should be held before school begins. Academic Conferences visibly demonstrate. Academic conferences should be calendared into the school schedule interspersed throughout the year. Many schools hold their academic conferences after students take grade-level benchmark assessments. This way teachers and leadership team members can review and process up-to-date student data in order to track progress and identify areas of success. It is amazing that a few effective academic conferences held throughout the year will develop unity, transparency, and trust. When academic conferences are held consistently throughout the school year they create a systematic method for changing school culture. Let's see how a principal would typically schedule classroom academic conferences into the school's calendar.

Calendar for Classroom-Teachers Academic Conferences

- ❖ **September - Classroom-Teachers Academic Conference #1**
- ❖ **November - Classroom-Teachers Academic Conference #2**
- ❖ **February - Classroom-Teachers Academic Conference #3**
- ❖ **May - Classroom-Teachers Academic Conference #4**

The accumulated planning, reflecting, and follow-through from the academic conference sessions will enhance instructional leadership and improve student learning for districts, schools, classrooms, and students.

Some things to consider:

- ❖ **Hold the conferences approximately four times a year.**
- ❖ **Hold the first conference at the beginning of the school year.**
- ❖ **Many schools hold the conferences after district benchmark testing.**
- ❖ **Hold the conferences during the school day for 30-40 minutes each.**

Academic conferences can be held during the school day with a rotating substitute teacher covering classes for 30-40 minutes. While teachers participate in the collegial conversations, the substitute can make sure students are continuing to work in class. When is the best time to start academic conferences? The simple answer: NOW.

<u>Why</u> are Classroom-Teacher Academic Conference so Powerful?

As professional educators we need to have pointed conversations about our students so that we can meet the academic needs. Many of these conversations happen out in the school parking lot, over the lunch table, or in teacher's lounge, yet they rarely happen in a supportive setting with relevant data. Classroom-teacher academic conferences help develop the leadership capacities of both the teacher leaders and school leaders.

Leadership Capacities Developed through Academic Conferences:

- ❖ **Instructional Leadership** (Developing dynamic classroom instruction)
- ❖ **Trust and Confidence** (Guiding their own academic destiny)
- ❖ **Interdependent Collaboration** (Working together to learn from others)
- ❖ **Independent Thinking** (Generating academic solutions)

Classroom-teacher conferences develop our instructional leadership, while building trust and confidence between team members, vertical alignment of the schools vision and collaboration will increase, and ultimately the independent thinking and empowerment of teachers will increase. Consider the following statements from school and teacher leaders:

"In the academic conferences we got a lot of things done. We established goals, developed plans, focused on students, and made commitments to continue our progress." **7th grade teacher**

"We really talked about students in what felt like a one to one conversation about the kids in each teacher's classroom." **Elementary Principal**

"It helped create a sense of urgency and it helped us to organize our instructional priorities." **1st Grade Teacher**

"We were able to see a lot of growth in the teachers and in ourselves as leaders when we looked at the data for our kids and reflected on the instructional practices and interventions that produced results." **Instructional Coach**

"The academic conferences were extremely beneficial because they followed a clear yet open format that focused on the particular needs of my classroom and my students." **3rd Grade Teacher**

Academic conferences benefit students, teachers, principals, and support staff in achieving the learning objectives for the entire school organization.

Academic Conference Template

A key component that contributes to effective conferencing is the academic conference classroom-teacher template. The template provides a clear framework for dialoguing and discussing about the instructional progress that is happening with students in the classroom. The classroom-teacher template begins by noting the important roles of chief contributor (teacher), facilitator (principal or other trained facilitator), and supporters (key staff members). The rest of the template is dedicated to highlighting the five conferral processes of reflecting, analyzing data, planning, creating solutions, and finally making commitments. The template provides space for the facilitator to initiate the Focus Question and encourage academic reflection by the chief contributor (the teacher may reflect about whichever aspects of instruction they believe will be helpful to improving student learning). Next, the template outlines the data to be analyzed and there is space provided to identify the five students the teacher will specifically track for instructional progress over the next several weeks (any five students may be selected by the teacher to track specific progress). The template then encourages dialogue about future instructional planning, and it provides space for the chief contributor to identify three plans to work on in the classroom. Let's now take a look at the classroom-teacher academic conference template.

Academic Conference Template

Chief Contributor		Date	
Facilitator			
Supporters			

❶ Reflecting:

Focus Question (Facilitator):

Reflection (Teacher):

❺ Analyzing Data:

Data Analyzed (Facilitator):

Identify Five Students: *(Chief Contributor):*

Name	Target/Needs
1	
2	
3	
4	
5	

❸ Planning: Set Three Goals

1	
2	
3	

(OPTIONAL) Creating Solutions:

Providing Suggestions *(Facilitator):*

Creating Solutions *(Chief Contributor):*

❶ Making Commitments *(Facilitator + Chief Contributor)*

Professional Growth Area (Chief Contributor):

Make Commitment & Confirm Teacher Commitments (Facilitator):

The next part of the template addressing creating solutions is optional (teachers as the chief contributors may not feel they need to discuss brainstorm and discuss new solutions). The final and in many ways the most important part of the conferencing template is making commitments. The chief contributor or teacher identifies their professional growth area, and the facilitator identifies an appropriate commitment for supporting the teacher's professional growth. Finally, the conference ends with the facilitator confirming the three commitments the chief contributor plans to implement in the classroom (the follow-up to the commitments may be the most powerful part of the conferencing process.)

How Do You Do It?

We have yet to consider the most important question of all for academic conferences—the how question. While the template provides a format and structure to the academic conference, it is a flexible tool designed to support reflection, independent thinking, and interdependent action. The facilitator should feel free to be flexible in how they use the classroom-teacher template to help guide academic conferences. They can jump around to different parts of the conference template emphasizing various aspects of the conferral process and spend more time on one conferral process over another depending on the interests and needs of individual teachers. The supporters (counselors, instructional coaches, psychologists, etc.) should leave each conferral session with greater insights into how they can support teachers and their students over the next several weeks. And most importantly, each classroom teacher as the chief contributor of their conferral dialogue should leave the conference session with an increased awareness of academic data, instructional plans, and classroom commitments for improving student learning. We will go into specific detail and more depth in Chapter Four regarding the key processes that make successful classroom-teacher conferences. For now let's take a peek back at our vignette from earlier in this chapter.

…Ms. Adams let out a sigh of relief and a smile crept across her face as she walked back to her classroom. Overall things went very well, and she didn't get fed to the

lions after all. In fact she felt a bit rejuvenated. She wondered how to describe the experience to her fellow teachers. It felt good to really talk about her students and how they were doing. She rarely had the opportunity to share the challenges that each of her kids faced in the classroom. She wanted every one of them to have a great year, and the planning, reflecting, and problem solving covered in the academic conference felt like it would truly make a difference. With the support of the school leadership team, she knew she would have the help needed to meet the academic challenges her students faced. As she returned to her classroom, she felt she had a clearer plan of action, additional intervention strategies, and a greater commitment to increase the achievement for each one of her students.

Summary

In these times, it is even more essential to engage in Academic Conferences to ensure that the collective efforts of individual educators will successfully contribute to the core mission, goals, values, and instructional interventions of the school organization. Conferencing allow us to plan and reflect on our professional practices and organizational progress. The classroom teacher serves as the chief contributor to the conference session, while the school principal typically serves as the facilitator of the conference. Academic conferences provide a forum for teachers and leaders to make sure that our students do not slip through the cracks, gaps, and chasms. They support a school culture of self-directed learning and collegial cooperation in behalf of students and the challenges they face. The conferences develop true ownership or internal accountability for the actions that teachers and administrators take towards instruction. We need to embrace a system for developing ownership where individuals at all levels *personally commit* to making changes that will affect the progress of student learning. Academic conferences help school leaders and teacher leaders become self-directed learners as we work together to improve instruction. Conferring together supports interdependent leadership where every educator plays a valuable role in working together to create solutions for kids. As we embrace the opportunity to work collegially as a team and align our common purposes in our profession, then our students will benefit the most.

Reflection Questions:

1. *How can Academic Conferences help your school organization and develop instructional leadership within the members of your organization?*

2. *What are the potential benefits for implementing Academic Conferences in your school and district?*

Chapter Three:

Supporting Classroom-Teacher

Academic Conferences

"Reflection can be a challenging endeavor. It's not something that's fostered in school - typically someone else tells youhow you're doing! teachers are often so caught up in meeting the demands of the day, that they rarely have the luxury to muse on how things went."

Peter Papas

Mr. Williams thanked Ms. Adams for her candid and insightful conversations about her students. A small smile seemed to escape from her lips as she concluded the thirty minutes conferral session and headed back to class. Mr. Williams looked around and asked the support staff "So, how did our first academic conference go?" Everyone was quiet until Ms. Taylor mentioned, "Even though Ms. Adams seemed a little nervous, I noticed that she started to really open up and share a lot about the her learning plans and progress she wants for her students in the coming months." Mr. Jordan added, "It looks like Ms. Adams is gaining additional perspective from the student data for what can be done for her students to master grade level standards." Mr. Williams leaned back and thought the dialogue was helpful and targeted on student progress. He felt this was a big step towards where their school needed to go. It was refreshing to feel like their time together was making progress; that they were going somewhere. But how would the next conference session go with one of the veteran teachers of the school?

Supporting Instructional Leadership

It is important that we spend time discussing the academic progress of our students. Academic conferences provide a venue for focusing on the instructional leadership needed for our schools. We expand our instructional leadership capacities as we openly reflect and consciously consider the academic progress of their students. When the instructional practices and academic progress within each classroom are brought to the surface and shared with one another, then everyone will benefit. Instructional practices that go unshared or are only shared between grade level peers can now spread to all teachers via the academic conference. Classroom-teacher academic conferences are much more than just getting together and chitchatting about things; they are about developing instructional leadership. As coaches and consultants, we (the authors) have had the opportunity to observe many conferencing sessions over the years. It takes a surprisingly small amount of time, but unless there is a clear focus, the time spent meeting can ramble on in ways that do little to contribute to instructional outcomes. Academic conferences provide the freedom for teachers to influence the conversation. That said the principal and leadership team should structure conferences to ensure that things stay on track. So, let's tackle just how a conference is done step-by-step.

Academic Planning

Our school systems typically have no real forum for focusing on Academic Planning. The district often does budget planning, construction planning, operational planning, compliance planning, personnel planning, etc. Rarely is there any academic planning that reaches down to the school level beyond gathering a collection of teachers together every couple of years to decide on a new curriculum adoption. If the district does have an instructional plan, it typically sits on a shelf at the district office gathering dust. The average teacher has little to no idea what any district instructional documents may say or how they should affect their everyday interaction with students. We need to take the time and devote our energies to creating an academic plan. While the district may do budget planning, construction planning, operational planning, compliance planning, and personnel planning, it is the academic planning and execution of that plan that will ultimately

Conferral Processes in Classroom-Teacher Academic Conferences

Academic conferences provide a forum for transforming our schools and they focus everyone's energy on those processes that will improve student learning. Many students need cohesive instructional actions that will intervene and address their specific academic needs. When principals and district administrators actively confer with those who know our students best (classroom teachers) and coordinate their instructional processes, we can save our struggling students by smoothing over the cracks, bridging the gaps, and carrying them out of academic chasms.

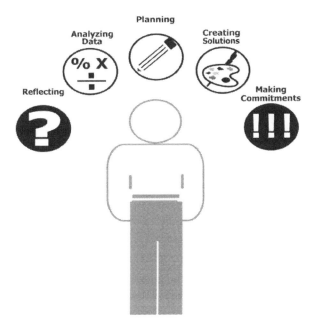

Figure 3.1: *The chief contributor selects from five conferral processes as they share their instructional insights in the academic conference.*

The Feedback Spiral is the primary model for the academic conference. The components of a feedback spiral may be diagrammed as a recursive, cyclical pathway with the following elements:

- ❖ **Reflecting on Instruction**

- ❖ **Analyzing Classroom Data**

- ❖ **Setting Classroom Plans and Goals**

- ❖ **Creating Classroom Solutions**

- ❖ **Making and Confirming Commitments**

So let's take a look at the five key conferral conversations that provide the main structure of the classroom-teacher academic conference.

Reflecting

Reflecting on Instructional Practices – The academic conference begins with reflection on instruction. The chief contributor or classroom teacher should reflect on academic performance, lessons learned, and insights gained or any other insights that shed light on the instructional experiences with students. We learn things at a deeper level, when we take the time to reflect on that experience. As we reflect on our educational experiences, we can use them to influence our future performance.

"Reflection requires space in the present and the promise of space in the future."
(Smith 1994, p. 150)

The purpose of reflecting is to provide us the time and format for real reflection and actively infusing it into our academic results. The focus question asked by the facilitator helps guide the reflection on instruction in the classroom. While the focus question should be asked in a way to help direct reflection, the teacher should feel free to bring up and share any reflective thoughts that shed light on how instruction is progressing in the classroom.

Analyzing Data

Analyzing Student Data – As teachers and principals our understanding of student needs will increase as we look at the quantitative data (formal assessments, state tests, exit exams, unit tests, etc.) and the qualitative data (classroom observations, survey results, student writing, etc.) to inform our instructional decisions. This data analysis and dialogue about improving future results is vital to increasing academic growth. Anderegg (2007) notes that,

"Professional development in data analysis for teachers must be directly applicable to their daily practice and linked to specific instructional objectives and goals."

The purpose of Analyzing Data is to consider objective feedback and see what can be learned about past instructional experiences and what can help influence future instructional activities. The data typically looks at the broader picture of how the class is doing. The chief contributor selects five students to focus their efforts over the next eight weeks or so. This intensive focus provides a qualitative aspect to the progress that is made. Focusing on data provides the academic conferences with feedback and insights into what may work with English Language Learners, struggling readers or other types of students that may need particular attention.

Planning

Planning Academic Goals – Planning creates a stage for the teachers to clearly understand the goals of the school and to establish their own goals that will meet the needs of their individual students. When do district administrators look at the specific needs of school sites? The standard answer is to have a multitude of meetings regarding budgets, operations, and maintenance. We must have a place to sit down and discuss our academic efforts and results. Andy Hargreaves (1998) notes that,

"In some ways, involvement in planning activity is more important than

producing plans—it is through collective planning that goals emerge, differences can be resolved and a basis for action created."

The purpose of Planning is to establish goals or outcomes that the teacher will focus their instructional efforts. The classroom teacher should identify at least three specific instructional goals that will improve student learning. This is one area where the goals may be academic, emotional, and social; the facilitator should only suggest possible goals, if the teacher asks for assistance in establishing classroom goals.

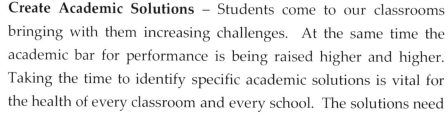

Creating Solutions

Create Academic Solutions – Students come to our classrooms bringing with them increasing challenges. At the same time the academic bar for performance is being raised higher and higher. Taking the time to identify specific academic solutions is vital for the health of every classroom and every school. The solutions need to come from those closest to the challenge. In our classrooms, that is the teacher. When we focus on solutions rather than problems, we are able to view students in positive light (Christensen, 2012). The purpose of creating solutions is to engage in a dialogue about challenges that teachers find perplexing as they strive to support student learning. This step in the academic conference is optional. The facilitator can provide ideas as to solutions that may be needed to help the classroom move forward to support the learning outcomes for the entire school organization. The key is to avoid focusing on students as problems and instead view the collective efforts of learning as a potential solution of improved outcomes.

Making Commitments

Make Academic Commitments – Finally, we need to be open and transparent about the academic priorities and commitments we will make to improve student learning. Academic conferences provide a format for making and following through on commitments. These commitments are made by teacher-leaders in the classroom, and by principal-leaders in our schools. When everyone meets eight weeks later for the next conference we can review the progress made on our commitments. The following statements demonstrate the power of an academic conference practiced correctly. When we have the autonomy to choose the plans and commitments we make, then the result is a much higher rate of achieving tangible results (Rock, 2010). The purpose of making commitments is to make sure that efforts moving forward are clearly have commitment and can be followed up in subsequent conversations, observations, and future academic conferences. The teacher outlines one professional growth area that they would like to focus on facilitator to make a commitment to the chief contributor that supports a professional learning development. The teacher states at least one are for professional growth that they will work on over the next several weeks, and the facilitator makes a commitment to support the professional growth area. The final step of the academic conference is for the facilitator to confirm with the chief contributor the three plans outlined are in fact commitments that they will work diligently on over the next several weeks to improve student learning.

Creating Collaborative Results

Academic conferences can bring together the important players in the school, and it provides them a frequent forum for really addressing the needs of students and the school. Consider the following diagram that highlights the important individuals who make the academic conference successful.

Classroom-Teacher Academic Conferences

Conferral Processes & Roles

Conferral Processes	Facilitator (School Administrator or Team Member)	Chief Contributor (Teacher)	Supporters (School Staff)

Reflecting	<u>Ask 1</u> <u>Essential</u> <u>Question</u>	Reflect on Instructional Practice	Listen Intently
Analyzing Student Data	Review Student Data for all students	Analyze Student data and <u>select 5</u> <u>students</u> to focus efforts	Record Information
Planning	Assist the teacher's thinking by questioning and listening	<u>Make 3</u> <u>plans</u> <u>to</u> <u>improve</u> <u>student</u> <u>learning</u>	Record Information
Creating Solutions	As needed help the classroom teacher create solutions	As needed work to create solutions for instruction	Listen Intently
Making Commitments	<u>Make 1</u> <u>Commitment</u> <u>to support</u> <u>teacher</u> and improve growth	Confirm the 3-pronged plan and commit to implement the plan	Provide support

Figure 3.2: Classroom-teacher academic conference chart of roles

Academic Conference places the principal, assistant principal and other site leaders squarely into an instructional leadership role. It positions them as a leader of academic conversations that will make a difference for kids.

The Conferral Feedback Process

The overall purpose of the academic conference is to create an open dialogue about the key factors that can lead to improved instructional practice, insightful understanding, and educational outcomes. When teachers and support staff engage consistently every eight weeks in the five conferral processes, the result is a cycle of continuous improvement in many of the areas that lead to increased professional and learning results. On their own, the processes of the feedback spiral are powerful in their own right. Reflecting develops a great depth of mutual understanding. Analyzing data develops greater insights into the current reality and opportunities for future progress. Planning and setting three goals creates powerful commitments. Creating solutions builds more confidence, and lastly making and confirming commitments creates common bonds and relationships between all involved. Yet, when the conferral processes are woven together the result is even more powerful. It should be noted that it may take an entire year of conferences to cycle through each phase of the feedback spiral. At the end of the year, the professional stakeholders will have a clear plan and understanding of student data and have solutions and ongoing commitments that will sustain academic success. Classroom-teacher Academic conferences provide the principal, school leadership team, and the classroom teacher with the ability to really review areas of success and identify opportunities for improvement. The conferencing will help to align programs and determine their effectiveness. In addition, the time spent together will help people become more unified in their understanding and in their resolve to do whatever it takes to improve student learning and classroom instruction. Schein (2004) observes that,

> *"The key to learning is to get feedback and to take the time to reflect, analyze, and assimilate the implications of what the feedback has communicated. A further key*

to learning is the ability to generate new responses; to try new ways of doing things and to obtain feedback on the results of the new behavior."

Academic conferences provide school and school districts with an effective forum for engaging in feedback spirals that improve academic results. The feedback spiral is a recursive process that frames the important dialogue, discussion, and conversations for instructional leaders.

Academic Conference Feedback Spiral

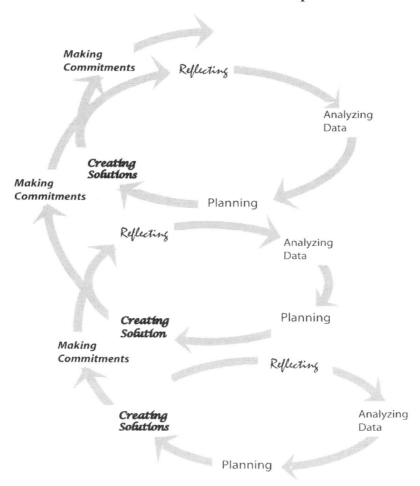

Figure 3.3: *The Conferral Feedback Spiral provides the key processes that produce results through academic conferences.*

The feedback spiral is a recursive process that frames the important dialogue, discussion, and conversations for instructional leaders. With three to four academic conferences a year, the feedback spiral provides the framework for improvement that lasts and forms a foundation for further improvement. The feedback spiral is fully complete when every student is learning at grade level and demonstrating they are proficient. Academic feedback spirals rely on a variety of data sources to inform the success of the school organization. As teachers, principals, and support staff engage in the conferral feedback spiral they will over time become better instructional leaders. Their ability to collaboratively reflect, analyze data, plan, create solutions, and make common commitments will increase.

Summary

Classroom-teach academic conference harness the academic energy in our schools just as the nuclear core harness the physical energy contained in an atom. The conferences serve as a unifying force that creates a cohesive academic program. Academic conferences build on several of the major movements of the last decade Professional Learning Communities, Response to Intervention, and Data Driven Analysis, as well as tried and proven practices of professional development and classroom observation. The ultimate benefit may be the cumulative understanding as the major work of school is coordinated over time. Academic conferences for Classroom-Teachers help us take on the many educational challenges that currently confront us. Classroom-teacher academic conferences provide classroom teachers and school principals with a forum for meeting the needs of all students. Classroom-Teacher academic conferences make a difference for teachers and students, because they serve as the primary mechanism that will drive our profession pursuit for quality instruction and student learning. It can be effective to coordinate Classroom-teacher academic conferences in conjunction with benchmark assessments that are provided throughout the school year. Conferencing provides the opportunity to piece together the personal growth, professional collaboration, and powerful intervention aspects of successful classrooms and schools.

Reflection Questions:

1. *When is the time and space provided to talk about the core issues that affect instruction and student learning in the classroom?*

2. *How can academic conferences improve the implementation, capacity building, and sustainability of academic initiatives in your school?*

Chapter Four:

How to Conduct Classroom-Teacher

Academic Conferences

"Education is a kind of continuing dialogue, and a dialogue assumes, in the nature of the case, different points of view."

Robert Hutchins

Ms. Matthews was pleased to hear that the principal and school support team would meet regularly with her to discuss the instructional needs in her classroom. What a novel concept! She was initially reluctant to talk with the school administrative team about the needs of her students, yet as their 35 minutes together passed things felt great. As the senior member of the teaching staff, it was nice to reflect on the past few months' progress. Talking about data and student results with the administrators helped her recognize where she should devote her efforts for continuing improvements. The conversations led by the principal seemed like the type of conversations an instructional leader should have about student learning. It would be nice to share her instructional plans and potential solutions for the future. The principal and support team promised their help. She was unsure if the next academic conference in eight weeks would go as well, but she anticipated the support from her for the plans she had for her students. It was exciting to think about the instructional leaders of the school understanding and working with her as the instructional leader of her classroom.

Strengthening Classroom Cultures

Academic conferences are a vital part of creating successful solutions and assessing academic progress for our students. What can we find in these conferences that directly help classroom teachers? Academic conferences overcome the three challenges that affect so many teachers. Conferences are designed to help educators establish their own clear expectations and design their work in ways that increases their internal capabilities rather than provide canned-solutions or externally "fix" others. Facilitators should shift their mental maps from *"How do I motivate others?"* to *"How can I create the condition in which they will be motivated themselves?"* Academic conferences help teachers and administrators reflect, plan, analyze data, create solutions, and make commitments. In addition to providing a broader perspective on our instructional practice, the academic conference also allows us to drill down to the very specific issues of individual learners. The academic conference honors the broad responsibility of attending to the needs of our schools and school system, while also honoring the specific responsibility of attending to the needs of the individual student. Thus, the framework influences the entire organization in a bottom-up approach, where the success of each individual student influences the success of the entire school structure. The end result of academic conferences is that they develop individual leadership capacities amongst teacher and school leaders. The entire organization benefits when individuals within our schools are able to better develop their own improvement processes. Harris & Lambert (2009) point out that,

> *"There would need to be a significant number of skillful teacher leaders who understood the shared vision in the school, the full scope of the work underway, and were able to carry it out. There would need to be commitment to the central work of self-renewing schools."*

Through the processes of self-managing, self-monitoring and self-modifying, teachers are more able to fully embrace self-directed learning and develop a greater internal locus of control. They increase their ability to manage the instruction in their classroom, monitor their behavior improve student learning.

We Have Lift-Off

Academic conferences serve as a vehicle for helping organizations create higher levels of collaboration and academic success for students. They allow the potential within individuals to laser in on the key processes that will help our classrooms and schools achieve results. Let's take a look at how this rocket ship for success looks like:

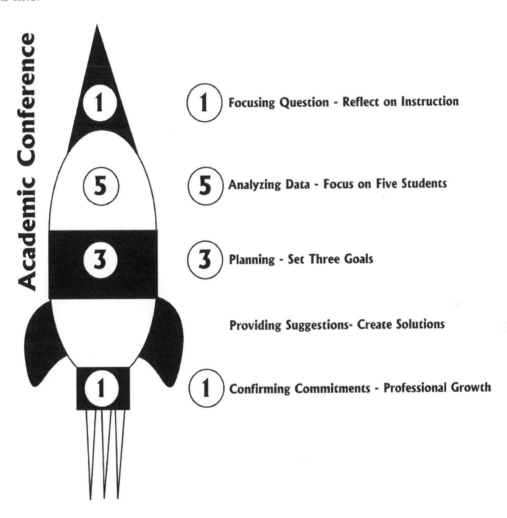

Figure 4.1: Academic Conferences are a vehicle for organizational achievement

The first step of every conference session is for the facilitator to ask one focusing question. This question should encourage reflection and thinking by the teacher as the chief contributor on how instruction is going in the classroom (Lipton & Wellman, 2000). Next, the facilitator helps analyze data and invites the chief teacher to interpret the results. To give a clear focus to the larger patterns data, teachers should identify five students that they will target for increased achievement over the next eight weeks. After reflecting on instruction and analyzing data, the teacher should identify three plans or goals that they believe will improve learning. The next step is optional; if teachers feel they need to create a solution they can dialogue and ask that the facilitator and supporters provide potential suggestions for solutions. The final step of the classroom-teacher academic conference is for the teacher to identify one professional growth area. In turn, the facilitator makes one commitment to support this area of growth, and they wrap-up the session by confirming the three goals that the teacher is committed to working on over the next several weeks until the next academic conference. Let's now take some time to go deep in depth with the five conferral conversations and take a look at some of the key concepts and example dialogue that will give us a better idea of the nitty-gritty aspects of conferencing.

The Five Conferral Conversations

At the heart of the academic conference are the five conferral conversations. These conversations focus the efforts of the teacher, principal, and members of the leadership team. The Five conferral conversations include:

- ❖ **Reflecting** – We learn from experiences, and we learn more when we reflect on our instructional experiences and share our insights with others.
- ❖ **Analyzing Data** – This conversation looks directly at the student data and provides a picture of how students are progressing.
- ❖ **Planning** – The planning conversation focuses in on the academic goals and instructional plans for each classroom-teacher.

❖ **Creating Solutions** – These conversations produces innovative solutions that lead to effective follow-through and real results.

❖ **Making Commitments** – This conversation builds ownership and provides a mechanism for measuring progress.

Every school-wide conference with classroom-teachers should analyze student data and conclude with specific commitments. Planning, reflecting, and creating solutions should be addressed as needed. For any successful conferral, the facilitator needs to be a great listener. When medical doctors prepare to address a health concern or outline a course of treatment, they begin by carefully listening to the issues of the patient. They listen to the qualitative insights as well as check some of the quantitative vital signs.

Reflecting Conversations

The Focus Question and subsequent reflecting conversations provide teachers with a time to reflect on how instruction is progressing for students. In order to ask quality questions, the facilitator needs to listen effectively in order to direct the conversation towards successful outcomes. The "Focus Question" provides direction to the train of thought for everyone involved in the academic conference. As teachers spend quality time with the school leadership team, the teachers will discover how the vision is progressing in each classroom with every student.

Focus Question Examples

- **"What are you doing to make sure that every student is academically successful?"**
- **"Which interventions are making a difference for our struggling students?"**
- **"What is working for the English Language Learners in your class?"**
- **"What seems to be the key instructional processes that are helping get the improvement in student learning in your classroom?"**

The primary tools that facilitators of academic conferences use are the skillful application of questioning. The chief responsibility of the facilitator of the academic conference is to ask quality questions of the classroom teacher. These questions should help surface the solutions that will work for each individual student. Becoming good at asking the types of questions that facilitate self-directed learning can take time and practice to master. The types of quality questions that guide academic conferences fit into several categories. It is an opportunity to identify strengths and areas for celebration of past successes. It is also a time for teachers to review areas for future improvement. Research by Marzano et al. (2001) show that the classroom teacher has the greatest impact on student learning and the school principal has the second most impact on student learning. It is important that these key individuals get together to collaborate and support instructional leadership.

Classroom Reflecting Conversations may include:

- ❖ **Responding to a "Focus Question" that supports reflection**
- ❖ **Sharing personal insights and perspectives of instructional practice**
- ❖ **Reviewing the commitments made previously**
- ❖ **Considering areas of strength**
- ❖ **Considering areas for improvement**
- ❖ **Reflecting on the coaching process**

Let's now take a look at a sample conversation for encouraging effective reflecting about classroom instruction:

Classroom Reflecting Example Conversation

Facilitator/Principal: *"How have your students done in meeting the grade level standards over the past six weeks?"*

Chief Contributor/Teacher: *"They've done very well on understanding the fantasy genre and their understanding narrative story structure. But... they are struggling a bit with their punctuation conventions."*

Facilitator/Principal: *"How did you do on the commitments you made from our last conferral session?"*

Chief Contributor/Teacher: *"Well, I made sure that every day the content objective was posted on the board and that the students recited it as a group, yet sometimes my checking for understanding was spotty."*

Facilitator/Principal: *"What is your impression about what caused two of your students to struggle?"*

Chief Contributor/Teacher: *"Both of them have some challenges at home. I will need to spend some more time with them in small group instruction."*

* Note that the deeper the reflection made by teachers in the conferral session, the greater the potential insights that may be discovered by the teacher.

Analyzing Data Conversations

Analyzing data conversations exist for interpreting data and building understanding of how students are doing academically. While conferences usually have enough time to cover a couple of the conferral conversations, the data analysis conversation occurs in most every conference because the students are present in the conference through data. The Classroom-Teacher conferences exist mostly to provide a stage for the teacher and the school leadership team to dialogue about specific students and how best to improve their learning. It is about the students, so the conference must address how to respond to the data.

The academic conference may be viewed as a qualitative inquiry where we clarify the perspectives, values, and insights of our professional colleague. To insure that the academic conference is practical and truly focuses on student learning, each teacher should select five students to focus the conversation upon. The classroom teacher should focus on five students that the teacher feels deserves additional attention. The teacher can point out the five lowest students, the five students who are ready to make a jump from below proficient to proficient, five English language learners and so on. Remember, it is about standards, not the story. It is more important to discuss how the student achieves the standards than the individual story that makes their progress challenging. The Academic conferences should focus on students—Special Education students, students who need universal access, struggling readers, students with difficulty in math, students who have faced recent emotional tragedy, gifted students, impulsive students, etc..

Classroom Analyzing Data Conversations may include:

❖ **Dialogue about Qualitative Observational Data**
❖ **Dialogue about Quantitative Assessment Data**
❖ **Interpret Patterns of Successful Growth**
❖ **Interpret Patterns for Future Focus**
❖ **Determine Key Points of Data to Improve Instruction and Learning**

Let's take a look inside a conversation regarding data and sub-group populations of students that may be deserving of specific attention.

Analyzing Data Example Conversation

Facilitator/Principal: *"What is our data saying about the seven English learners in your classroom?"*

Chief Contributor/Teacher: *"Most of them are doing okay in math. But understandably, they are struggling a bit in English and Language Arts."*

Facilitator/Principal: *"Uh-huh".*

Chief Contributor/Teacher: *"I'm thinking about trying more small-group interventions with my English language learners."*

Facilitator/Principal: *"So you feel that small group instruction will make a difference?"*

Chief Contributor/Teacher: *"Yeah. I feel they need more attention and more time to support their understanding and language development."*

Facilitator/Principal: *"So now that we have looked over the data which five students are you going to focus on for the next eight weeks?"*

Chief Contributor/Teacher: *"I think I want to focus on the high end and the low end. I'm going to focus on Kimberly and Bryce, two of my struggling readers. And Jose, Berta, and Sergey are my three newest English language learners."*

Facilitator/Principal: **Okay.** *"What do you want to do for them?"*

Chief Contributor/Teacher: *"I want to provide more enriching activities to extend Kimberly and Bryce's thinking and I want to provide scaffolded language support for my three ELLs."*

Facilitator/Principal: *"I look forward to hearing how things progress."*

*Looking at disaggregated data of student sub-groups like ELL's and Title I students can help focus on trends. In addition, focusing on five students can highlight specific student needs.

Classroom Planning Conversations

The planning conversation is a conferral with the purpose of establishing goals, plans, and objectives of the teacher that will meet the academic needs of students.

This type of conversation often occurs in academic conferences at the beginning of the school year. This is an ideal time for the instructional leaders of the school to identify clearly stated plans for improving student learning. Looking over student data can assist in determining academic targets.

Make Three Plans or Goals

As teachers develop their confidence in making and keeping their academic plans or goals, they will begin to stretch themselves and their students to achieve more than they would have previously been able to foresee. It is important that the commitments are written down. The commitments may be small or they may seem quite significant. The key is that the instructional leader supports the teacher in the achievement of the three commitments that they believe will benefit student learning.

Classroom Planning Conversations Include:

- ❖ **Dialogue regarding standards and student's needs**
- ❖ **Clarifying of school goals and classroom objectives**
- ❖ **Establishing written goals and objectives**
- ❖ **Determining what the outcomes will look like**
- ❖ **Discussing how you will know when you have achieved the stated goals and objectives**

As we look at an example of a classroom planning conversation, we should note that planning between instructional support staff and classroom teachers can create powerful academic results.

Classroom Planning Example Conversation

Facilitator/Principal: *"What are your top goals and objectives?"*

Chief Contributor/Teacher: *"I want to make sure that all of my students leave my class having mastered their grade level standards."*

Facilitator/Principal: *"What do you want your students to be able to do when they leave your classroom at the end of this next eight weeks?"*

Chief Contributor/Teacher: *"I want all my kindergarten students to know how to count to a hundred."*

Facilitator/Principal: *"What do you want your students to be thinking or feeling when the class is done for the day?"*

Chief Contributor/Teacher: *"I want them to think about how they can become better writers and feel that they have the confidence to achieve it."*

Facilitator/Principal: *"So what commitments are you ready to make for your students?"*

Chief Contributor/Teacher: *"I will shake each student's hand as they enter class to strengthen our relationship. I will provide more writing activities to my students. And... I will meet with each student to go over their annual assessment scores."*

Facilitator/Principal: **Okay.** *"Those all sound terrific. I look forward to hearing about the progress that your students will make."*

Chief Contributor/Teacher: *"I hope that you will come by in a couple of weeks to look at the writing."*

Facilitator/Principal: *"I will bring my sticky-notes and comment on their writing. Thanks again for all that you do for our kids."*

Chief Contributor/Teacher: *"Yeah, thanks."*

*When teachers are purposeful, specific, and transparent about their academic plans with support staff, then there is an increased likelihood of achieving superior results.

Creating Classroom Solution Conversations

This conferral step is optional in the conference session. Only if teachers feel they need support in identifying a classroom solution, does the facilitator engage in this process. The ultimate purpose is for the teacher to come up with new ideas and solutions as they have time to consider and reflect. The facilitator helps by asking probing questions, pausing to listen, and paraphrasing the thinking of the teacher. If at the end of this process, teachers are still unable to identify a workable solution, the facilitator should only then offer three suggestions or potential solutions that the teacher can then select from as a possible path to pursue. It is important that whatever course of action or solution that is identified, that the teacher ultimately makes the final decision. When potential solutions are determined by the teacher rather than dictated by administrators, the success of the solution increases significantly (Rock, 2010). A primary purpose of academic conferences is to create solutions for the educational challenges that students face. Each teacher brings valuable insight and intelligence to academic conferences.

Solution Creating Conversations may include...

❖ **Dialogue about the desired need**
❖ **Share Potential Solutions**
❖ **Decide on a Course of Action**
❖ **Work together to achieve Solution results**
❖ **Check back to see ways the Solution can be sustained**

Let's consider some dialogue for creating collaborative classroom solutions that can benefit student learning:

Creating Classroom Solutions Example Conversation

Facilitator/Principal: *"It looks like you've identified four of your seventh graders that are struggling to read at grade level."*

Chief Contributor/Teacher: *"Yes. They can't keep up social studies, science or literature and it's really affecting their learning."*

Facilitator/Principal: *"So what do you think will make a difference?"*

Chief Contributor/Teacher: *"Well, I've talked to the other seventh grade teachers and we all have several students that are struggling and we're not sure what to do about it."*

Facilitator/Principal: *"Well what do you think will work?"*

Chief Contributor/Teacher: *"Frankly, I was hoping that the leadership team would give me a solution."*

Facilitator/Principal: *"What intervention ideas have you brainstormed so far?"*

Chief Contributor/Teacher: *"I've been so busy trying to cover the content and I've checked with the other teachers. I really could use a suggestion or two."*

Facilitator/Principal: *"Well let's see what we can do then. For one: you could consider explicitly teaching the four different types of text structure. Or two: you could front load the key academic language that are part of the lesson's reading assignment that they might be unfamiliar with. Does anyone else on the leadership team have a suggested reading intervention?"*

Participant/Instructional Coach: *"You could also teach the students about "signal words" that reveal text structure."*

Facilitator/Principal: *"Do any of those ideas sound like they'd work for your students?"*

Chief Contributor/Teacher: *"I really liked the first suggestion. I think that could really work for my kids. Can I get some more information on the different types of text structure? I could use some help on how to integrate that into my lesson plan."*

Facilitator/Principal: *"Definitely! I will follow through and help in this area."*

*While this part of the conferencing process is optional, when there is sufficient time devoted to creating workable solutions this can be one of the most beneficial aspects of the conference session.

Rather than a "problem-solving" conversation, academic conferences embrace solution-creating conferral where the focus is shifted from the problem and on to the solution. Often problem-solving conversations get fixated on the problem and can only see potential solutions through the lens of the problem. Solution-creating conversations look to identify solutions wherever they may be found. As we work together to create innovative solutions to the challenges our student's face, we will grow as professional colleagues. Classroom-teacher conferences provide the time to explore solutions and identify effective practices.

Commitment Making Conversations

Commitment making conversations clearly establish which direction instruction will go in the classroom. This portion of the academic conference makes sure that the ultimate result is a clear call to action. Every conference ends with a commitment making conversation, including the 5 – 3 – 1. This way the professional stakeholders at the school have a clear idea of where instruction is headed for students. As commitments are made, teachers and principals alike can work together to achieve these aims. The actions generated from the commitments create a cohesive dynamic that pulls people together. After making plans, analyzing the data, reflecting, or creating solutions, the conference concludes with clear commitments. It is important that these commitments are reviewed during future conference conversations. The follow-through is what makes the academic conference a success. The commitments should be reviewed during the reflection portion of the next academic conference.

> **Commitment Making Conversations may include...**
>
> ❖ Outlining a professional growth area
> ❖ Dialogue regarding plans and commitments that will benefit student learning
> ❖ Confirming the commitments for growth and progress
> ❖ Putting commitments down in writing
> ❖ Following through on commitments and progress
> ❖ Celebrating successful commitments achieved

Confirming Commitments

A grade level PLC may decide that they want to explore the same topic and then share their findings with one another. Just as the teacher makes three commitments, the instructional leader should commit to supporting the teacher in the professional growth area they select. These are "I will..." statements made by the principal. They demonstrate a return commitment to the teacher that focuses on areas of professional growth for the teacher. We often say that we value life-long learning, yet do we actually demonstrate that value by consistently coordinating our learning? Probably less than we would like.

Making Commitments Example Conversation

Chief Contributor/Classroom Teacher: "I am unsure if I am leading small group instruction effectively. I could really use some new ideas."

Facilitator/School Principal: "I am willing to do a couple of things. I can observe your small group instruction and provide feedback, order a book about Response to Intervention (RTI) for each member of your grade level, or I can send you to an RTI conference. What would work best for you?"

Chief Contributor/Classroom Teacher: "I could use some training on engagement strategies to get my students more motivated."

Facilitator/School Principal: "I will be happy to get you signed up for an upcoming workshop, if you will come back and share what you learn with your professional learning community (PLC)."

Chief Contributor/Classroom Teacher: "Great! I will start looking for a training that will make a difference for my kids."

Let's look over another example of a commitment making and commitment confirming conversation:

Making Commitments Example Conversation

Facilitator/Principal: "So as we look at your five students that you're targeting, what are your three commitments that you are willing to make for the next six weeks?"

Chief Contributor/Teacher: "Um…Well since it's the beginning of the year and I've got a hundred and eighty new ninth graders that I want to build relationships with, I will shake their hand as they enter the classroom every day for the next six weeks. And, I'm going to give them the opportunity to do an essay on something they are passionately interested in. And I think I want one to be focused on improving their academic results."

Facilitator/Principal: "So what do you think would work there?"

Chief Contributor/Teacher: "Hmmm… I want to improve the results on the benchmark assessment by ten percent for my students that are scoring at below basic."

Facilitator/Principal: "Do you feel good about these commitments?"

Chief Contributor/Teacher: "Totally. I can do this, but some support would help."

Facilitator/Principal: *"I'll check in with you about how the handshakes are affecting relationships and see how the essays turn out. I'll have the instructional coach provide any support for helping you with the test results."*

Chief Contributor/Teacher: *"Thanks. That'll be great. I appreciate it."*

*It is important for us to make consistent commitments in our instructional practice and to monitor our progress towards these commitments. The needed commitment is a commitment to experiment, not necessarily a commitment to quantitative results. Try new strategies and new ways of thinking. Be willing to reflect back on the experimental process. At the next academic conference, the commitments can be reviewed and lessons learned can be shared.

Classroom-teacher academic conferences follow a simple formula that keeps the focus on kids in the classroom, on personal commitments, and on tangible support and follow through. It sets the stage for consistent progress in the classroom and a successful conference in another eight weeks. Now that we are seeing all of the components of an effective conference, let's look at an example template that will help guide the chief contributor, facilitator, and participants to success.

Classroom-teacher Academic Conference Follow-Up

Following the academic conference a short abstract should be written up by the teacher to summarize the goals and commitments. The academic conference for teachers use the development of the abstract writing process as a means of reflection and review of their commitments. The academic conference is a time and place to allow the best thinking to come to the surface. Schools have a vast resource of thinking talent, yet it seems that this thinking talent is rarely tapped in a way that helps student learning with a comprehensive, systematic method. Our schools languish because some of the best thinking in schools never makes it beyond the classroom level. We have islands of excellence that are not shared. The conferral creates an environment for contributors to focus on and share their best thinking. Let's take a look at a classroom-teacher academic conference template filled out.

Classroom – Teacher Academic Conference Form

Chief Contributor	Mrs. Adams – Classroom Teacher		Date	September 20th
Facilitator	Mrs. Williams – School Principal			
Participants	Mr. Thomas - Assistant Principal, Pam Smith - School Counselor, & Georgia Peters - Psychologist			

❶ Reflecting:

Focus Question (Facilitator): "How are your students progressing academically?"

Reflection (Teacher): Key Points - Most of the students are doing well and they are on target. ELL students still need interventions and support. Student writing is improving.

❺ Analyzing Data:

Analyze Data (Facilitator)
- English Benchmark Data, Mathematics Benchmark Data, & Student Writing Samples

Identify Five Students: *(Chief Contributor)*

	Name	Target/Needs
1	Samantha Williams	Sam needs help in academic language vocabulary and pronouncing his "r" sounds
2	Charlie Bowen	Charlie needs help blending and segmenting multi-syllabic words accurately
3	Jose Vargas	Jose has limited academic language vocabulary and speaks infrequently in class
4	Julietta Lopez	Julietta needs help in numeracy confidence and particularly multi-digit multiplication
5	Peter Vang	Peter struggles with his fluency rate in decoding and with his prosody

❸ Planning: Set Three Goals *(Chief Contributor)*

1	*Commitment #1: I will do 30 minutes of small-group instruction every day for 4-6 students who need additional help in fluency, vocabulary, phonics, etc.*
2	*Commitment #2: I will develop weekly instructional plans with Professional Learning Team and share practices that are producing positive results.*
3	*Commitment#3: I will post at least one example of each student's work on classroom walls each week.*

(OPTIONAL) Creating Solutions:

Creating Solutions (Chief Contributor): "Things seem to be going well so I don't have any major solutions for now."

Providing Suggestions *(Facilitator)*: "Great to hear, let's now confirm our goals and commitments."

❶ Confirming Commitments *(Facilitator + Chief Contributor)*

Identify One Professional Growth Area (Chief Contributor):
Growth Area: "It would be great to get some additional support in the area of ELD Strategies to help me meet my Hmong student's needs."

Make Commitment and Confirm Teacher Commitments (Facilitator):
Commitment support from the principal: "I will stop by the classroom once a week to look at student work and provide sticky-note comments on at least 3 students to acknowledge their learning & growth."

Increasing Classroom Teacher Assets

Conferencing helps develop teacher, classroom, and school success. Through classroom-teacher conferences, teachers will become more meta-cognitively aware, more reflective on their expertise and experience, and more creative in their thinking and understanding. Effective classroom-teacher conferences develop the instructional leadership, confidence, and thinking of each teacher.

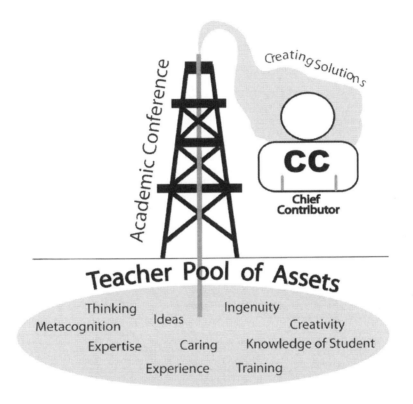

Figure 4.2: *The academic conference help teachers tap into their many assets that highlight their talent as instructional leaders.*

Academic conferences place the teacher in the important role of an instructional leader. Classroom-teacher conferences value the thinking, expertise, and experiences of the teacher. They draw out the caring, creativity, and knowledge that seldom receives opportunities to surface. As teachers, we go about our business every day and rarely do we get the opportunity to share the understanding we gain about our students. Academic conferences provide a process for our best thinking to surface and our best ideas to be recognized and appreciated. Standard teacher evaluations try to judge the talents of a teacher by looking at a few short observations. In contrast, academic conferences are designed to value the expertise and experience teachers bring to the profession, and help develop the instructional talents of every teacher.

Summary

Academic conferences for Classroom-Teachers provide us the opportunity to discuss student learning. They give teachers and school principals a forum to openly dialogue about the key issues affecting quality instruction. Conferencing focuses the professional stakeholders on the "Essential Questions" that face the school and classroom. The strategic vision and key initiatives can be transferred from the district boardrooms down to the school classrooms. The academic conference provides the time to achieve the key elements and purposes. Conducting academic conferences allows participants to orchestrate the best thinking to be expressed and implemented. As the facilitator (usually the principal) asks quality questions, the chief contributor (teacher) is able to create solutions and improve instruction for students. Conducting Classroom-Teacher academic conferences several times throughout the school year will build trust and confidence between the professionals on the school campus. The results have the power to transform instruction and learning for everyone. The 5-3-1 format keeps a focus on kids, a focus on improving instruction, and a focus on teacher development.

Reflection Questions:

1. *How can academic conferences for classroom-teachers transform the dialogue and discussion that occurs in our schools?*

2. *Which of the five types of conferring processes was your favorite? Why?*

Chapter Five:

Leading School-Administrator

Academic Conferences

"The real methodology for system change begins and ends with ongoing authentic conversations about important questions."

Tony Wagner

Mary walked the halls of her school and wondered how the students were really doing. Were the kids really learning in the classrooms throughout the day? She chatted with her teachers about student behavior in the cafeteria, yet it seemed the things she really wanted to talk about never happened. Yes, she had the one or two hours a year to evaluate the teachers in the classroom, yet it was such a quick snapshot of the real picture that it seemed to be a superficial review of instruction and learning. So much emotion was wrapped up into this formal evaluation that it seemed little was really accomplished. How she wished that she could just sit down with her teachers and listen to how the students were doing overall. As she observed in the classroom she had several quick snapshots of how the students were doing, yet she also wanted to know how the teachers felt things were going. It appeared some students were struggling while others seemed to be doing well. She decided that she would sit down with each teacher and really listen to their current concerns and future plans for success in the classroom.

Pursuing a Common Vision

Our profession as educators in many ways is at a crossroads. As we strive to generate solutions to our collective challenges, we need to find ways to work together towards a shared vision. Aligning everyone together around a shared vision takes both time and understanding. A clear pathway can only be developed as we work together as true professionals and develop a unity of purpose. As instructional leaders, we need to work together to strengthen the foundation of education as a professional field. Our school systems need to operate in ways that support learning and increases our ability to become instructional leaders. As school leaders, we need a plan and a consistent process for infusing a successful academic vision and coordinating the academic results throughout our entire school organization. For our schools to improve, we *must* have the opportunity to embrace a vision and give voice to the professional work behind our instructional plans, perspectives, and practices. Otherwise, whole groups of students will continue to struggle. We need to keep the primary purposes of school—*student learning and quality instruction*—at the forefront of our school efforts. The instructional initiatives, academic plans, and district vision statements all need to align to the everyday actions of everyone charged with improving learning outcomes. The key individuals that are responsible for school-wide success—principals, and district administrators—need to address the ever present issues of student learning and instruction.

Outlining a Shared Vision for Our Schools

Our schools and district organizations need a clear vision to guide the instructional efforts of everyone within the organization. The primary task of the district's leadership team is to establish and communicate a clear vision for quality instruction and student learning. Every school district has the important responsibility of outlining for its members the vision and values of the organization. Whether it is called a *"strategic vision"*, *"district vision"*, or *"school board vision for improvement"*, this vision is a crucial part of directing the energies of everyone involved in the organization. Academic conferences provide the perfect venue for communicating and creating accountability for the organization's academic vision. In our educational systems it seems there is a never ending list of operational procedures, yet little time to truly discuss instructional progress. As a result the important educational vision of the district never seems to get implemented in a consistent and cohesive fashion. At the same time school principals never really gets the support they often need to propel their school forward. Open and transparent discussions about instruction can mutually support the vision of the district, the insights of the principal, the values of the teachers, and the best interest of our students. Senge and colleagues (2000) observe that,

"In building shared vision, a group of people build a sense of commitment together. They develop images of 'the future we want to create together,' along with the values that will be important in getting there and the goals they hope to achieve along the way."

Developing a shared vision requires conferring and collaborating between district leaders and site administrators. School district leadership needs to give careful consideration to how this vision is communicated and aligned with the efforts of each individual school within the organization. It seems many district leadership teams spend substantial effort and time crafting a quality vision, only to see this vision posted on the district website never to be discussed or heard from again. The most important aspect of a school vision for success is that it is a shared vision. It takes a conscious effort on the part of district leaders to ensure that the vision is aligned with the important leaders of schools and classrooms. Mission and vision statements, however, are not just exercises in articulating desired outcomes. They should become active efforts for reflecting, analyzing data, designing plans, creating solutions, and making commitments. A school's mission statement is given substance and value when it is systematically compared to current progress.

School-Administrator Academic Conferences

Academic conferences do a tremendous amount to add value and bring together the various aspects of the school district organization. The school administrator academic conference is the vehicle for creating instructional leadership at the district level and school level that will drive student learning to higher levels of achievement. Academic Conferences allow the organization to shift from first gear, to second gear, into third gear, into fourth gear, and eventually into fifth gear as they identify needs and then step up to meet the ever pressing academic needs. Establishing clear priorities that are regularly reviewed and discussed will increase results for the entire organization. Dufour and Marzano (2011) p. 34 state that,

> *"Central office leaders must not only clarify those priorities but should be vigilant in monitoring the degree to which the priorities are understood and acted on throughout the district."*

Many schools go down the highway of learning stuck in a low academic gear. They want to shift into a higher gear, yet they need the support to really kick things into overdrive. At the same time, academic conferences for school administrators held at the district level set the tone for the entire organization and give greater purpose to everyone's efforts. While school-wide academic conferences align classroom practices and purposes with the school's instructional leadership purposes, district-wide academic conferences align school practices and purposes with the district's instructional leadership purposes.

School and District Needs

School

Academic conferences are structured to support learning conversations and at the same time create a high-quality learning organization. Will there be a day when district administrators, site administrators, and teachers work together as true colleagues? The language of academic conferences is important because Regenerative Language helps create an environment where things can grow and flourish. In order to achieve these four purposes of District-wide academic conferences, the chief facilitators must create a culture and environment that feels psychological safe. The facilitator wants to create a positive emotional state where the chief contributor feels pulled towards a positive state. This has also been called a towards-state of feeling or a reward sense. The following statements demonstrate the power of an academic conference practiced correctly.

"In the academic conferences we got a lot of things done. We established goals, developed plans, focused on students, and made commitments to continue our progress." **7th grade teacher**

"We really talked about students in what felt like a one to one conversation about the kids in each teacher's classroom." **Elementary Principal**

"It helped create a sense of urgency and it helped us to organize our instructional priorities." **Middle School Assistant Principal**

"We were able to see a lot of growth in the teachers and in ourselves as leaders when we looked at the data for our kids and reflected on the instructional practices and interventions that produced results." **Elementary Instructional Coach**

"The academic conferences were extremely beneficial because they followed a clear yet open format that focused on the particular needs of my classroom and my students." **High School Principal**

School and District Leadership

The mission statement, strategic initiatives, and focus question frame the dialogue and discussion of academic conferences. Together they impact reflection, planning, commitments, and solutions in powerful, yet subtle ways. The facilitator may refocus the conversation by referring to the mission statements or strategic initiatives. Academic conferences expand the individual principal's perspectives to connect with the broader goals of the school and connect with the specific goals of the individual student. The dual objectives of our profession are considered—

contributing to both the profession of comprehensive education and the profession of personalized education. Truly professional educators are able to contribute to both the profession of the broader educational system and the profession of educating the individual student. Often times district administrators get caught up in filing reports and administrivia, and they lose focus of the primary purpose of school—learning.

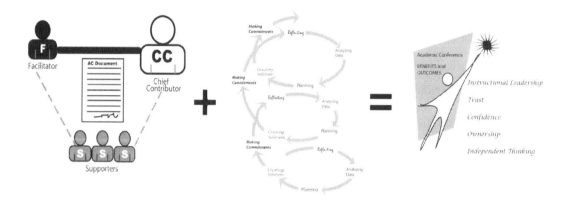

Figure 5.1 - Here is another look at important processes in Academic Conferences

School-administrator academic conferences provide a clear focus for district leaders and site leaders to meet and discuss the academic progress of schools and students. Aligning the vision, interests, and actions of everyone in the school organization allows it to move forward effectively and efficiently.

Vertical Alignment within School Organizations

School-administrator academic conferences connect the vision and leadership of the district with the leadership and implementation of school administrators.

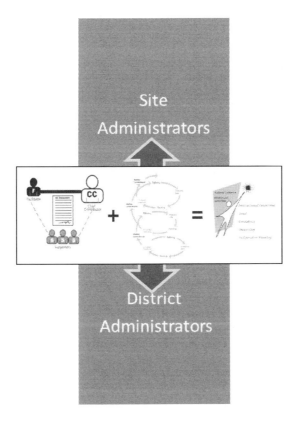

Figure 5.2: *School-Administrator*

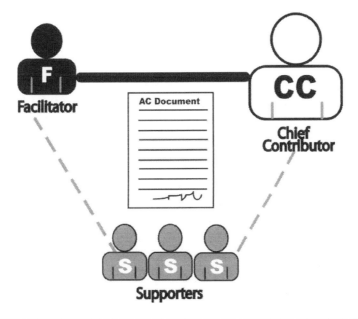

Figure 5.3: *The primary roles in a School-Administrator Academic Conference are Chief Contributor, Facilitator, and Supporters.*

School- Administrator Academic conferences are needed to align the actions of schools with the objectives of the district and this type of conference helps keep the focus on student learning and quality instruction. School-administrator academic conferences are needed to align the actions and efforts of schools with the organizational values and initiatives of the district.

Roles and Relationships in School-Administrator Conferences

The roles established in academic conferences are designed to enlist the best thinking of everyone at the table. We have the ability to create solutions to the challenges that face our students. The relationships in academic conferences need to be made safe by encouraging open dialogue and frank discussion of student data results and their specific needs. There are three main roles at the academic conference:

❖ **Facilitator** (Assistant Superintendent or other District Administrator)
❖ **Chief Contributors** (School Principal & Site Leadership Team)
❖ **Supporters** (District Directors)

The most important aspect of the academic conference is to strengthen the relationships of those who have responsibility for student learning. Our roles overlap and we have a collective ownership to work as interdependent leaders in behalf of our students. We live in a day when isolated efforts will most often fall short of meeting the learning demands of our students. Developing these relationships in ways they can flourish takes a different approach than most typically considered. Let's take a quick look at each of the three roles outlined in school-administrator academic conferences. We will take a more in depth look at the specific responsibilities of these roles as we talk about them in the upcoming chapters.

Facilitator's Role – School-Administrator Conferences

The facilitator sets the stage for the academic conferences success. The district superintendent or assistant superintendent of instruction typically fills the role of facilitator at school-administrator academic conferences. As a facilitator their role is to guide the conferral conversations forward. As they effectively interact with the chief contributor (principal & school leadership team) they can help bring innovative thinking and creative solutions to the surface.

Facilitator

Figure 5.4 – The Facilitator for School-Administrator Academic Conferences is typically the district's Assistant Superintendent of Instruction.

The facilitator creates an atmosphere of trust where ideas can be shared, instructional plans can be made, student data can be analyzed, solutions can be developed, and commitments are made. Schein (2004) notes that leaders of successful schools model and exemplify the skills which create a culture of inquiry,

> *"The important lesson here is that teams almost always work better when the higher status person in the group exhibits some humility by active listening; this acknowledges that the others are crucial to good outcomes and creates psychological space for them to develop identities and roles in the group that feel equitable and fair."*

There is a lot of expertise and skill that facilitators bring to the table when conferring, yet there are four process skills that are essential to facilitating effective academic conferences.

Facilitator Key Skills

- ❖ *Asking Focus Question*
- ❖ *Analyzing School Data*
- ❖ *Encouraging School Plans*
- ❖ *Suggesting Solutions*
- ❖ *Confirming Commitments*

Typically the principal assumes the facilitator role at the classroom-teacher academic conference, yet anyone who is trained in the key processes of facilitating can fulfill this role.

Chief Contributor's Role - School-Administrator Conferences

In school-administrator conferences the chief contributor is the school principal and school leadership team primary individual who influences the academic conference. As we consider the challenges that face our schools, we know that the principal is the most important individual to the success of the school (Marzano et al., 2001). The ultimate success of the academic conference hinges on the chief contributor gathering the understanding that is gained, solutions that are created, and commitments that are made and then taking the actions to improve academic progress.

Chief
Contributor

Figure 5.5: *The Chief Contributor of School-Administrator Academic Conferences is the School Principal*

The chief contributor is the most important individual at the academic conference, because they know the most about what is going on in their primary area of responsibility—the school organization. In addition, the skills of reflection, analysis, planning, solution creating, and committing to purposeful action are the key processes that make academic conferences so powerful in achieving results for kids.

Chief Contributor Key Skills...

- ❖ *Reflecting on School-wide Instruction*
- ❖ *Interpreting School Data*
- ❖ *Setting School Plans*
- ❖ *Creating School Solutions*
- ❖ *Making Commitments*

The school principal is the chief contributor in the school-administrator conference. The chief contributor engages in dialogue and discussion with the facilitator in order to develop plans, solutions, and ideas for improving instruction and student learning. The chief contributor provides the primary direction, issues, and actions to be discussed at the conference. The principal is the Chief contributor at the district-wide academic conference for school-leaders.

Supporter's Role – School-Administrator Conferences

Supporters play a support role in the school-administrator academic conference. The most important role the supporters play is to listen to the chief contributor (school principal), so that they can understand additional ways to support them. Supporters may take notes as needed to record the plans, solutions, and commitments made during the conference sessions.

Supporters

Figure 5.6: *Supporters school-administrator conferences*

While supporters play a quiet, yet important role in the academic conference, their most lasting impact typically occurs through the actions they take to support their colleagues after the conference session. Supporters will learn a lot by being present at academic conferences.

Supporters Key Skills

- ❖ *Listen Intently*
- ❖ *Record Information*
- ❖ *Provide Support*

In the school-administrating academic conferences the key supporters are usually directors of instruction, special education, English Language Learners, etc. The supporter's role in the conference is to listen and learn how they can better support individual teachers in the classroom and individual schools in the areas where they need it most. Supporters really provide their support by the actions they take after the conference session is over. They should take the information they glean and use it to provide targeted support in areas that support teacher instruction and student learning.

There are five key processes that direct the flow of the conference. The key processes include:

- ❖ Reflect on School Instruction
- ❖ Analyze School Data
- ❖ Plan and Goal Setting

- ❖ Create Solutions
- ❖ Make Commitments

We will explore in greater detail in the next chapter. For now let's look at how the key roles interact with the key processes for school-administrator conferences by considering the following chart:

Academic Conferences for School Administrators

Key Roles and Conferral Processes

Conferral Processes	Facilitator (District Asst. Sup. or Team Member)	Chief Contributors (School Principal & Team)	Supporters (District Staff)
Reflecting	Ask (1) Essential Question to facilitate Reflection	Reflect on the school's Instructional Results and Progress	Listen Intently
Analyzing Student Data	Review the school's Student Data and with the classroom teacher	Analyze the school's student data and select (5) areas of focus	Record Observations
Planning	Assist the teams	Make 3 pronged	Record

	thinking as they develop a 3 pronged plan	plan to improve instruction for the school	Observations
Creating Solutions	As needed continue to help administrator team create solutions for the school	As needed seek assistance in creating solutions to improve instruction	Continue to Record Observations
Making Commitments	Make 1 Commitment to support the administrator team	Confirm 3-pronged plan to implement the instructional plan at the school	Provide support

Figure 5.7: *Comparing key roles to the key processes of school-administrator conferences*

District Planning

It is important that every school district have a clear instructional plan that is discussed with school leadership teams and in turn with classroom teachers. The major component of successful districts, schools, and classrooms are taking the time to thoughtfully plan. The district creates the climate which shapes the context for common instructional purposes, while the principal helps select the specific areas that the school and district will pursue together. Academic conferences provide a forum for everyone to focus on instruction in a systematic, yet flexible method. Conferencing becomes a co-creative process that allows innovation and interest to flourish. The academic conference at the district level provides a forum for the district to meet, plan, review, and celebrate the academic progress of the schools. It keeps the focus squarely on students and their classroom successes.

<u>Who</u> are the Major Players in the District-wide Academic Conferences?

The academic conference pulls together the major players of the school district together and puts them in one room with the responsibility of talking specifically about student learning. Conferences help showcase school successes and zero in on areas for instructional improvement.

District Superintendent – The superintendent should lead the academic vision of the district. Academic conferences are an excellent way that the superintendent can stay connected to the academic results of each school and ensure that each school is making progress. Superintendents attend academic conferences and ask questions, yet the facilitator role is typically left to the assistant superintendent of instruction.

Assistant Superintendent of Instruction - The assistant superintendent most often facilitates the meeting and is primarily responsible for keeping the dialogue and discussion focused on student needs and their learning progress.

Directors of Curriculum, Professional Development, Special Education Assessment, etc. – Directors that are responsible for academics attend academic conferences and serve as supporters of the school administrator academic conferences. They take the information they glean from these meetings to help guide their academic support after the conferral sessions.

School Principal – The principal with the help of the school leadership team serves as the chief contributor of the school administrator academic conference. The principal and the school leadership team prepare presentations, anticipate questions, provide a power point, bring examples of student work, and review the schools initiatives in coordination with the districts academic initiatives.

Assistant Principals – For schools with an assistant principal, they should also play an active role in the Academic Conference. The can prepare data, run the LCD projector or document camera, and showcase student data and work.

Academic Coaches – Can offer suggestions, reinforce ideas. Take notes and record the needs of the teacher and individual students. The instructional Coach can use this information to truly support the teacher in ways that the teacher finds to be most helpful.

Students represented by data – Students are the primary focal point of academic conferences. While they are not physically present at the conference, they are represented by data, classroom work, and vital information showcasing their academic performance.

The school-administrator academic conference places the principal, assistant principals, and other site leaders squarely into an instructional leadership role. Conferences position these folks as leaders of the academic conversations that will make a difference for kids. Now that we have briefly outlined the major players of these conferences, let's consider some other important components to designing effective conferral sessions.

<u>What</u> potential topics should be covered in the School-Administrator Academic Conference?

School-administrator academic conferences emphasize the vision and values of the school district. The key initiatives of the district should be reviewed and discussed. Major sub-group student populations should be considered like English Language Learners, Title 1 students, special education students, etc. School-administrator

Conferences are a time of academic discovery where the instructional vision is shared and becomes a shared vision for the entire organization. This is a time to emphasize and dig deep into what the district values and taking the time to align these values with the values of each school. The questions that the assistant superintendent asks will guide the direction of the conversation and keep the dialogue and discussion.

School Data – Take the time to look at school data in a variety of areas. State assessments, benchmark assessments, demographic data, school surveys, and other information can be analyzed and used to provide feedback to organizational progress.

Common Core State Standards – What do the grade level standards look like in each core content area. How is the school doing to implement the standards?

Curriculum – Is the core curriculum being used as designed? Is it meeting the needs of students? What adjustments may need to occur to make a difference for students?

Instructional Practices – What instructional methods and strategies are being used at the school to create results? How are students responding to various instructional practices?

Academic Interventions – What interventions are in place at the school for English Language Learners, struggling readers, and students with special needs?

Ultimately the district vision along with the implementation efforts of each school is the major

<u>Where</u> should School-Administrator Academic Conferences be held?

The Academic Conference should be held in a location where there will be no disruptions and the district staff and school leadership team can interact comfortably. Sitting at a round or rectangle table where everyone can be at the table is important. The conference space should allow for a projector where up-to-date student data can be displayed for everyone to review.

- ❖ *A quiet comfortable setting away from distractions. Usually in the districts board room.*
- ❖ *A space where everyone (district staff and school leadership team) can be at the proverbial table*
- ❖ *A space where a projector can display school data*

The school-administrator academic conference should provide the space and time for instructional leaders (principal, assistant principals, instructional coaches, etc.) to look at the data and discuss student's needs at each individual school.

When should the District-wide Academic Conference be Held?

These district-wide academic conferences are typically held four to five times a year to support school-leaders, yet they can be held as frequently as needed. The first academic conference for each school year should be held before school begins. Academic conferences should be calendared into the district's schedule interspersed throughout the year. Many districts hold their academic conferences after schools take grade-level benchmark assessments. This way district staff and school leadership team members can review and process up-to-date student data in order to track progress and identify areas of success.

Calendar for school-administrator academic conferences (Held at district office)

Let's review several of the things to consider when calendaring in Classroom-teacher Academic Conferences:

- ❖ *Hold school-administrator conferences about four times a year*
- ❖ *Hold the first conference at the beginning of the school year*
- ❖ *Many districts hold the conferences after district benchmark testing*

❖ *Hold school-administrator conferences for about 60-90 minutes for each school*

Looking at individual student data contributes to the quality of the learning conversations regarding student progress.

Holding school administrator academic conferences help create buy-in to key district initiatives.

<u>Why</u> is the School-Administrator Academic Conference so Powerful?

As professional educators we need to have pointed conversations about our students so that we can meet the academic needs. Many of these conversations happen out in the school parking lot, over the lunch table, or in teacher's lounge, yet they rarely happen in a supportive setting with relevant data. Classroom-teacher academic conferences help develop the leadership capacities of both the teacher leaders and school leaders. Consider the following capacities that are developed through effective conferences:

Organizational Capacities Developed through Academic Conferences

❖ *Interdependent Leadership*
❖ *Trust & Confidence*
❖ *Academic Ownership*
❖ *Independent Learning*

Each of these four organizational capacities will improve the overall performance of the school district. Interdependent leadership develops as key administrators talk openly about how instruction at each school site is going. Trust and confidence is built as everyone involved recognizes that instruction and students are the key focus of administrators throughout the district. In upcoming chapters, we will talk more about the benefits of school-administrator conferences and why we should use them to support instructional improvement in our districts.

Academic Conference Template

Chief Contributor		Date	
Facilitator			
Supporters			

① Reflecting:

Focus Question (Facilitator):

Reflection (Teacher):

⑤ Analyzing Data:

Data Analyzed (Facilitator):

Identify Five Students: *(Chief Contributor):*

	Name	Target/Needs
1		
2		
3		
4		
5		

③ Planning: Set Three Goals

1	
2	
3	

(OPTIONAL) Creating Solutions:

Providing Suggestions *(Facilitator):*

Creating Solutions *(Chief Contributor):*

① Making Commitments *(Facilitator + Chief Contributor)*

Professional Growth Area (Chief Contributor):

Make Commitment & Confirm Teacher Commitments (Facilitator):

Summary

The outcomes generated by academic conferences help us align our learning goals, apply the instructional vision, account for academic results, and take action in constructive ways. Academic conferences allow the organization to address the internal challenges and external challenges that confront our schools and students. Our school districts and their leadership teams have the primary responsibility for designing and disseminating a clear academic vision for principals, teachers, students, and community members. The vision should be clearly focused on student learning and quality instruction. Most school districts have taken the time and effort to develop some type of vision statement. Some districts have even taken the time to develop a strategic vision. The documents outlining the district's strategic vision are often prominently posted on the district's webpage. The academic conference provides the time and process to establish a shared vision, to align the organizational values, and to encourage the personal voice of each professional within the organization. The Superintendent and other District Administrators are often keen communicators of the vision, yet they often have limited opportunities to communicate this vision to those who implement the vision principals and teachers. Effectively conducted academic conferences make sure that the purposes, practices, and plans of the district are effectively implemented in the classroom. The academic conference gives district leaders the time and forum for making sure that the district vision is well articulated and aligned with the understanding of site leaders, and academic conferences give site leaders the opportunity to see that the vision is aligned to the understanding of classroom leaders.

Reflective Questions

1. *How does your school ensure that the vision of district leadership is embraced and becomes a shared vision within the organization?*
2. *How do innovative ideas and successful practices get consistently communicated within the organization?*

Chapter Six:

Key Principles of School-Administrator

Academic Conferences

"Learning organizations are characterized by total employee involvement in a process of collaboratively conducted, collectively accountable change directed towards shared values and or principles."

Watkins & Marsick

George finished the report on his desk before leaning back in his chair and glancing out the window. He wondered how the district could really make the growth that the students were capable of making. Taking the job as superintendent in this small town had been a big move. Let's face it, he was taking a risk, yet the board was also taking a bit of a risk on an enterprising young leader who had done an excellent job as a principal was now in charge of a small district of 3,200 students. He wanted to bring all of the district staff into a collegial focus on his two top priorities: student learning and great instruction. How could he get everyone to see their important role in accomplishing these priorities, while at the same time develop their skills and talents? He had heard about academic conferences providing a forum and focus for transforming school culture. He decided that he needed have his district staff and site administrators trained in conducting conferences effectively. The promise of his district staff working better with site principals, and site principals working more closely with classroom teachers on instruction seemed worth the gamble.

Creating a Learning Organization

The primary purpose of School-Administrator Academic Conferences is to create a learning organization that aligns the district's vision from top to bottom. They are designed to achieve the vision of the school district's leadership. Creating a learning organization requires regular learning conversations and structured collegial dialogue. In order to create a learning organization, learning conversations need to be at the heart of how the district and schools operate. In chapter three we noted the importance of learning conversations to support classroom effectiveness; in this chapter we highlight the importance of creating learning organizations to support school effectiveness. Cohen & Prusak (2001) note that effective learning organizations make,

> *"...appropriate organizational investments—namely giving people space and time to connect, demonstrating trust, effectively communicating aims and beliefs, and offering equitable opportunities and rewards that invite genuine participation, not mere presence."*

Effective learning conversations build learning organizations and effective learning organizations build the thinking and doing capacities of people in the organization.

School-Administrator Academic Conferences Establish Outcomes

Academic Conferences develop the vision, values, and goals of individuals and the organization, which in turn clarifies for individuals their academic identity and enhances the cultural identity of the organization. When School-Administrating academic conferences are conducted regularly, it helps everyone within the organization recognize their identity as influencers of student learning and contributors to quality instruction. The leadership of the district should establish goals and targets while articulating specific outcomes that the district organization wants to achieve. These goals, targets, and outcomes should align and be in harmony with the goals, targets, and outcomes that site leaders have established for their schools. And ultimately the districts goals should fit well with the goals, targets, and outcomes of teachers and students in the classroom. When does the organization ever take the time to make sure that goals, targets, and outcomes are established? Goals are the overarching objectives of the organization. The targets are specific results that can be measured. Individuals can more clearly recognize their role within the organization. They will appreciate that they are supported and student needs are met. Individuals within the organization will know that their ideas are accepted, their commitments are respected, and their actions are appreciated. In our current society, change is the current reality. Internal forces and external forces put our schools in a position of facing change. Three key qualities of leaders are they produce direction through vision, alignment through collaboration, and commitment through ownership (Van Velsor et al. 2008). Ultimately relationships will be strengthened as the organization achieves the goals they have collectively created.

School District Outcomes

Every school district has goals, purposes and outcomes that are important. One of the greatest barriers to school improvement are unclear and innumerable initiatives that are pursued by the district that lack coherence Achieving the goals of student learning and quality instruction takes a high degree of coordination and collaboration. There are five key goals, purposes, or outcomes which the district facilitator of a school-administrator conference is interested in achieving. These primary purposes include:

- ❖ Help School-Leaders prioritize the vision, initiatives, and plans for the school
- ❖ Help School-leaders reflect and make effective decisions for the school
- ❖ Help School-leaders diagnose and analyze feedback data

❖ Help School-Leaders create their own solutions for students
❖ Help School-Leaders make and keep commitments that benefit student learning

Like the classroom-teacher academic conferences, the school-principal academic conferences should focus on developing the self-directed learning skills of the chief contributor. In this case the chief contributor of the school is the principal and includes the school leadership team. When school principals get the opportunity to play the facilitator role in the classroom-teacher academic conferences, and they also get to shift roles and play the chief contributor role in the school-principal academic conferences. Playing both roles particularly helps school principals recognize what it feels like to be a chief contributor and a facilitator of academic conferences. These experiences will help school leaders better see how the questions, listening, pausing, paraphrasing, and positive presuppositions all contribute to increasing the self-directed learning of the school organization. Whichever instructional initiatives the district and school decide to pursue, the academic conference provides the forum for keeping the initiative on track. As a result, academic conferences become the unifying force that holds the instructional vision of the classroom, school, and district together. Now let's look at some of the who, what, when, why's, and wherefores' that make up effective academic conferences for the classroom-teachers at the school level. Garmston (2005) notes that,

> *"Leaders who learn publicly, are continuing inquirers, are confident enough that they can reveal thinking—in-progress—and are genuinely curious. These leaders can be the soul of inquiring cultures."*

Providing a forum for addressing the responsibility that we all have as educators to ensure our students are making consistent academic progress. Taking the time to dialogue develops understanding and carving out time for discussion strengthens instructional decisions.

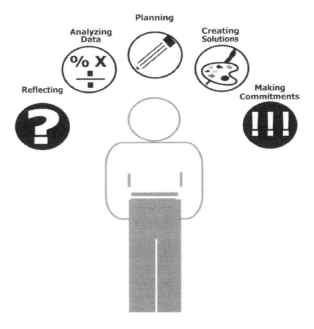

Figure 6.1: *The chief contributor selects from five conferral processes as they share their instructional insights in the academic conference.*

The conferral process is the primary model for the academic conference. The five components of conferring include the following elements:

- ❖ **Reflect on Instruction**

- ❖ **Analyze Data**

- ❖ **Plan and Set Goals**

- ❖ **Create Solutions and Modify Actions**

- ❖ **Make Commitments and Experiment**

Reflecting

Reflecting on School Practices – School-administrator academic conferences provide us the time for real reflection on how our schools are performing. As we consider our instructional efforts and academic progress, we will be better positioned to achieve the results we desire. Focusing our attention on the instructional process will give us insights and ideas that will fuel our future efforts. Schon (1983) notes that instructional leaders need to engage in,

> "...continuous professional reflection on the gap between the ideal state of proficiency and the present reality of a school."

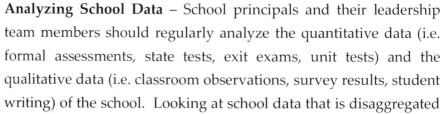

Analyzing Data

Analyzing School Data – School principals and their leadership team members should regularly analyze the quantitative data (i.e. formal assessments, state tests, exit exams, unit tests) and the qualitative data (i.e. classroom observations, survey results, student writing) of the school. Looking at school data that is disaggregated into the demographic sub-groups of the school makes sure that all students receive the attention and help they need. Analyzing sub-groups can help inform the instructional decisions for our schools. Looking objectively at data is vital to the academic growth and improvement of our schools and district organizations. Marzano (2003) emphasizes that,

> "If schools are in the business of helping students learn, then the data used to guide decisions should relate directly to student achievement"

Planning

Planning School Goals – Planning creates a stage for the school leaders to clearly understand the goals of the district and to establish school goals that will meet the needs of all students. School administrators should work collectively as a team to make plans or goals that they are committed to achieving. These plans should be written down during the school-administrator conference, so that follow through can occur at the next conference eight weeks later. While school administrators often meet with district administrators regarding budgets, operations, and maintenance, it seems that rarely is student progress specifically addressed. We must have a place to sit down and discuss our academic efforts and results. Costa (2007) notes that,

"Planning a strategy before embarking on a course of action assists us in keeping track of the steps in the sequence of planned behavior at the conscious awareness level for the duration of the activity. An example of this would be what superior teachers do daily: developing a teaching strategy for a lesson, keeping that strategy in mind throughout the instruction, and then reflecting back upon the strategy to evaluate its effectiveness in producing the desired student outcomes."

Creating Solutions

Create School Solutions – It seems that we face ever increasing challenges in our schools. Some of these challenges are external in nature (i.e. more English Language Learners moving into the community or less parental support) while other challenges are internal in nature (i.e. limited financial resources or new state standards). Solutions need to come from those closest to the challenge. In our schools, that is the school principal and leadership team. Creating effective solutions takes time to dialogue and consider. Typically potential solutions must be implemented before we are able to determine if they are effective. Zmuda (2010) observes that,

"A learning organization provides regular opportunities for learners to reexamine existing knowledge, assumptions, products, and processes to determine more innovative approaches, new areas of opportunity, and potential solution paths."

Academic conferences give us the time consider potential pathways for action and the space to create solutions as we reflect on the instructional process and make plans for improvement.

Making Commitments

Confirm School Commitments – The most powerful part of the school-administrator academic conference may be confirming the three commitments or plans that are made during each conference sessions. Public commitments provide a common understanding of our plans and our priorities. Academic conferences also provide a format for following through on commitments by scheduling to meet every eight weeks or so to discuss progress and reassess school commitments. Commitments can be instructional, social, curricular, assessment, or professional. Commitments empower us to pursue a path and to report back on our progress. While school administrators make the commitments, the leadership team will need to work with teachers, students, and the entire school community to achieve most commitments. Because these commitments are made by school leaders, it encourages greater ownership for the ultimate results of these commitments. Collins (2001) identifies effective leadership as one,

"...who catalyzes commitment to a compelling vision and higher performance standards."

These commitments are made in behalf of the school. As the chief instructional leader of the school, the principal should make commitments that focus the school. These commitments will vary from school to school within the district organization, yet they should all support the vision and values of the district. The commitments should be stated in a way that they can be verified by the district organization.

Inquire Humbly

One of the key elements for coordinating an effective academic conference is the quality of questions that the district leadership asks of the school principal and site leadership team. Questions that are effectively presented will engage principals in thinking that will provide creative solutions to the challenges our students face.

Effective Focus Questions...

❖ **have positive intentionality**
❖ **are open-ended**
❖ **seek clarification and specificity**

Let's take a look now at a sample of the academic conference template:

Academic Conference Template

Chief Contributor		Date	
Facilitator			
Supporters			

1 **Reflecting:**

Focus Question (Facilitator):

Reflection (Teacher):

5 **Analyzing Data:**

Data Analyzed (Facilitator):

Identify Five Students: *(Chief Contributor):*

Name	Target/Needs
1	
2	
3	
4	
5	

3 **Planning: Set Three Goals**

1	
2	
3	

(OPTIONAL) Creating Solutions:

Providing Suggestions *(Facilitator):*

Creating Solutions *(Chief Contributor):*

1 **Making Commitments** *(Facilitator + Chief Contributor)*

Professional Growth Area (Chief Contributor):

Make Commitment & Confirm Teacher Commitments (Facilitator):

As principals and school leadership team members ask quality questions of teachers, then an open dialogue can support the core academic issues in the classroom. Next we will look at how classroom-teacher academic conferences support instructional initiatives. Notice how sample questions are provided which demonstrate how the conferences can support various instructional initiatives and overall school improvement. Effective questions that are shared in the classroom-teacher academic conferences can produce results that support teachers, student learning, and quality instruction. It should be noted that it may take an entire year of conferences to cycle through each phase of the feedback spiral, and that they do not necessarily occur in a specific order.

Academic Feedback Spirals for School Leadership

In addition to benefiting instructional leadership at the school level, the feedback spiral process of academic conferences also benefits school district leadership. The number one thing the district leadership needs to provide is a shared vision of academic success. Student learning or academic success is the primary purpose that the public education organization exists. The number one thing they need to is accurate data that informs how the organization is progressing toward the purposes of student learning and quality instruction. Feedback spirals supported through academic conferences create a scenario where instructional leaders operate with a higher degree of rigor. W. Edwards Deming (2000) improved business organizations throughout the world and he emphasized the following processes that lead to organizational transformation.

> *"... A person and an organization must have goals, take actions to achieve those goals, gather evidence of achievement, study and reflect on the data and from that take action again. Thus, they are in a continuous feedback spiral toward continuous improvement."*

Learning organizations openly seek feedback and assess their collective progress. If you asked most district administrators if it is important, they would invariably say yes. The information gleaned from these formal conferrals provides valuable insights into the effectiveness of the organization. The academic conference embraces a consistent process that extends throughout the school year and continues into future school years to improve the instructional leadership of the organization. Let's take another look at the Conferral Feedback Spiral:

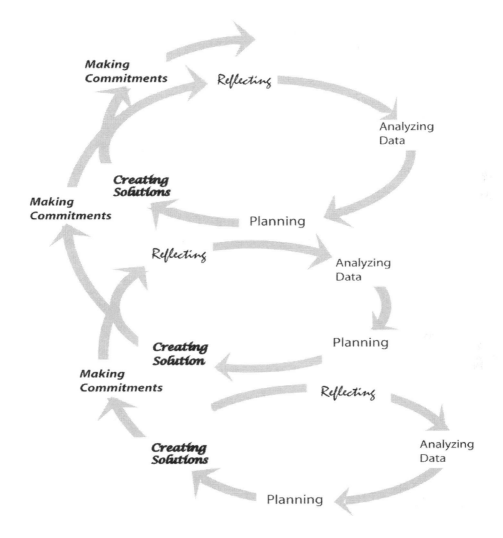

Figure 6.2: *The Conferral Feedback Spiral is also instrumental in guiding conferences for school-administrators.*

It should be noted that it may take an entire year of conferences to cycle through each phase of the feedback spiral, and that they do not necessarily occur in a specific order. At the end of the year, the professional stakeholders will have a clear plan and understanding of student data and have solutions and ongoing commitments that will sustain academic success.

Summary

School-Administrating Academic Conferences provide the principal with time to reflect on progress. Academic conferences clarify for the organization what will receive attention, what things mean, how we will emotionally respond to things, and what actions need to be taken to improve the organization. Academic conferences provide a stable and consistent process that is flexible to meet specific academic needs. Conferencing provides a feedback process that encourages change and progress that is anticipated and understood. Educational organizations are often highly charged with emotion, because of the anxiety that occurs because of accountability and change elements that are not clearly understood by those who have the greatest impact on the organization. It is within the academic conference that the theoretical ideas of central office meet the practical implementation of the school classroom. The vision and values of the organization need to be applied in classroom practices that will actually make a difference for individual teachers and students. The dialogue and discussion that occurs within district level academic conferences informs district leadership and clarifies the direction for school leadership.

Reflection Questions

1. *How does your district develop instructional leadership throughout the organization from top to bottom?*
2. *How can academic conferences help your district get the right data and feedback to insure individuals within the organization are accountable for academic results?*

Chapter Seven:

How to Conduct School-Administrator

Academic Conferences

"Learning organizations are characterized by total employee involvement in a process of collaboratively conducted, collectively accountable change directed towards Shared values and or principles."

Watkins & Marsick

George finished the report on his desk before leaning back in his chair and glancing out the window. He wondered how the district could really make the growth that the students were capable of making. Taking the job as superintendent in this small town had been a big move. Let's face it, he was taking a risk, yet the board was also taking a bit of a risk on an enterprising young leader who had done an excellent job as a principal was now in charge of a small district of 3,200 students. He wanted to bring all of the district staff into a collegial focus on his two top priorities: student learning and great instruction. How could he get everyone to see their important role in accomplishing these priorities, while at the same time develop their skills and talents? He had heard about academic conferences providing a forum and focus for transforming school culture. He decided that he needed have his district staff and site administrators trained in conducting conferences effectively. The promise of his district staff working better with site principals, and site principals working more closely with classroom teachers on instruction seemed worth the gamble.

Creating Shared Values

The values of the district are equally important as the vision. The district's values need to align with the values, beliefs, and assumptions of school principals and classroom teachers. Like a shared vision, taking the time to ensure that the values of the district become truly shared values is extremely important. A value like "Every student can learn" may be espoused by district leaders, yet in practicality is this value embraced by site leaders and classroom leaders? While it is important that a shared vision is supported by everyone within the organization, it is equally important that the organization develop a sense of shared values. As each individual embraces and reflects a common set of shared values, then the organization will be truly aligned. While a shared vision helps direct the quantitative interactions of the organization, shared values help direct the qualitative interactions of the organization. Garmston & Wellman (2008) relate,

> *"Values and beliefs about learning, collegiality, and relating to students and parents are all shaped by personal reflection and interaction with other professionals. Reflective dialogue serves the dual purpose of developing shared understanding and helping individuals to clarify personal thinking to ground their actions."*

The collective values or beliefs of the individuals within a school influence how the organization faces challenges. The academic conference provides a forum for dialoguing about beliefs and discussing values.

Conferring About Instructional Values

When our values are clear, the decisions we make are easy. School organizations develop integrity as key members perceive the congruence between its initiatives, vision, and mission with its daily practices. The Academic conference provides a forum for school leaders to impact the conversations that frame the culture of the school campus. The conversations can focus more on productive planning, solution creating, commitment making, and other positive dialogue and discussion that will support a positive culture. Christensen (2012) points out that,

> *"A key metric of good management, in fact, is whether such clear and consistent values have permeated the organization."*

Uplifting conversations lead to new perspectives that reshape and reframe the ways that we look at the culture of the school, and in turn this influences the culture of individual classrooms. When the vision and values become shared between individuals, then the entire organization will be aligned and efforts will work effectively together. Academic conferences allow the vision of the school organization to be fully understood and applied where it ultimately makes a difference—within the individual classroom and within individual students. When the instructional leadership at the district, school site, and classroom levels observe students, they can with assurance see the progress our students our making. Academic conferences must occur regularly throughout the school year. They initiate processes that are capable of transforming individuals each and every day, and thus they must happen on a consistent basis. Relationships are only built through consistency. Academic conferences are much more than just an ad hoc meeting thrown together throughout the school year. The sessions embrace a variety of focused processes that spiral through and transform the thinking and actions of the most important individuals in the success of our students—teachers, principals, and district administrators.

School Lift-Off

School-administrator conferences can serve as a rocket ship for school success. A district administrator facilitates the conference by asking a focus question that gets the school leadership team to reflect on progress made. The facilitator then reviews the school data with everyone as they interpret the data and look for patterns of achievement or patterns of need. The data should help inform the plans and goals that the school leadership team is prepared to commit to working on to improve learning results.

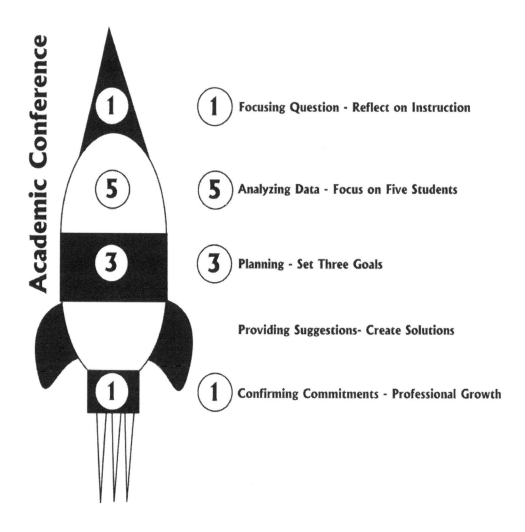

1 Focusing Question - Reflect on Instruction

5 Analyzing Data - Focus on Five Students

3 Planning - Set Three Goals

Providing Suggestions- Create Solutions

1 Confirming Commitments - Professional Growth

Figure 7.1: Academic conferences are a vehicle for school success.

Potential solutions can be dialogued as needed, and then the conferral session wraps up with the district leadership team making a commitment to support the needs of the school and the site leadership team. The school-administrator academic conference develops self-directed learners and it supports teachers taking ownership of their areas for professional growth and progress. The point of these conferences is to provide a place and time for the academic leaders of the school to have focused conversations that create real results.

School Reflecting Conversations may include:

- ❖ **Dialogue about Qualitative Observational Data**
- ❖ **Dialogue about Quantitative Assessment Data**
- ❖ **Interpret Patterns of Successful Growth**
- ❖ **Interpret Patterns for Future Focus**
- ❖ **Determine Key Points of Data to Improve Instruction and Learning**

Let's now take a look at a sample dialogue between a district facilitator and a high school principal about student learning:

School Reflection Example

District Facilitator: *"How are things at your school and what do you have to share with us today?*

Chief Contributor/Principal 9-12: *"Well, we are excited about our progress on our commitments from our last academic conference. We exceeded our target on commitment #1) Increasing benchmark scores in social studies by 10% over last year's scores. We met our target on commitment #2) Enrolling more students in AP classes' particularly low socio-economic students. And, we made some progress, yet we still need to continue working on commitment #3) Increasing by 20% the percentage of students who need to complete night school to graduate on time."*

District Facilitator: *"Say more about the success your school achieved on commitment #1 social studies benchmark scores."*

Chief Contributor/Principal: *"Our teachers really dug into the state standards and they did more role play and debates with students to get them engaged in the content. This emphasis resulted in a 16% increase in scores over last year's benchmark scores at this time."*

District Facilitator: *"Congratulations to you, your team, and all of your teachers and students. Please, pass the congratulations on for us. And, what made a difference for your school as you achieved commitment #2 more students enrolled in AP classes?"*

Chief Contributor/Principal: *"Our counselors and teachers worked together to target those students who scored well on the class and state assessments, and we sent out a letter to the parents and brought the students into the office to extend a personal invitation and tell the students we had confidence they could succeed. As a result we increased our AP enrollment by 77 students over last year, and 24 more low socio-economic students enrolled this year than last year."*

District Facilitator: *"Great for those students. Do you expect the passage rates on the AP exams to stay high also?"*

Chief Contributor/Principal 9-12: *"So far the teachers are saying the student's grades are good, and they believe the students are working together and progressing well.*

District Facilitator: *"What was learned as you worked on commitment #3, and what will you continue to do in this area?*

Chief Contributor/Principal: *"We have an increase of 14% of students on track to make up credits and graduate on time which is below our target, yet we feel good about the increase for our students, and Mr. Williams our night school teacher believes that our monthly meetings with parents will get us to the 20% by the end of the year with the parent support."*

District Facilitator: *"Thank you, we look forward to hearing how things continue to progress. Is there anything else your team has reflected on over the past eight weeks?"*

Chief Contributor/Principal 9-12: "Well, we are excited about debate team placing 3rd at the state tournament, and..."

* The time reflecting on academic progress will help lead to improvement going forward. The district leadership staff also benefit from hearing the insights and reflection of the school personnel who are leading instruction day to day.

Analyzing School Data Conversations

It is important for schools to assess academic progress so that student learning can be measured and evaluated. The school administrators should collect and review quantitative data as well as qualitative data. Quantitative date like formal assessments is extremely valuable to get feedback on how students are doing. At the same time, quantitative data that is collected and observed by classroom teachers is also important to review and consider. The progress for sub-group populations at the school should also be considered. Sub-groups of students that typically struggle should be given particular attention. English language learners, low socio-economic learners, struggling readers, and minority students are just a few of the sub-group populations that can be analyzed and reviewed. When we analyze data together as a district leadership and school leadership staff, we are able to

---

Analyzing School Data Conversations may include:

- ❖ **Dialogue about Qualitative Observational Data**
- ❖ **Dialogue about Quantitative Assessment Data**
- ❖ **Interpret Patterns of Successful Growth**
- ❖ **Interpret Patterns for Future Focus**
- ❖ **Determine Key Points of Data to Improve Instruction and Learning**

Let's take a moment to consider a sample of an analyzing data dialogue between school district leaders and a site administrative team.

School Analyzing Data Example

District Facilitator: *"What data did you bring with you today for us to look over?"*

Chief Contributor/Principal K-6: *"We have our third benchmark assessment scores in English/language arts and math compared with the third benchmark scores from last year for grades 2-6. We also brought and a sampling of fourth grade student writing and online assessment scores. We also brought attendance data for the past three years."*

District Facilitator: *"Thank you for all of this preparation. As we look over the benchmark assessment data in English Language Arts and Math and compare it to last years' results, what patterns do see standing out?*

Chief Contributor/Principal: *We are seeing significant growth in 5th and 6th grade math scores. Even though we went up in most grades in ELA, we saw a small decrease in 2nd grade ELA scores.*

District Facilitator: *"What do you think is at the root of these results?*

Chief Contributor/Principal: *"We believe that the district's initiatives are helping. The math training we had last summer for our teachers seems to be making a difference in math scores. An increase in English Language learners at our school may have affected our 2nd grade ELA scores, so as we have met with our teachers in our classroom-teaching academic conferences, we believe an increased emphasis in training and support for ELL's will help."*

District Facilitator: *"Thanks for sharing. Is there anything else that you believe may be affecting our 2nd grade ELA scores?"*

Chief Contributor/Principal: *"We need to focus in on our segmenting and blending skills along with frequent reading time and fluency development for the 2nd graders."*

District Facilitator: *"As we look over the 4th grade student writing, what do you see?"*

Chief Contributor/Principal: *"Our students are doing a good job with conventions and punctuation, yet we believe we can see improvements in transition sentences and support for the main topic."*

District Facilitator: *"Anything else you and your team are thinking about data?"*

Chief Contributor/Principal: *"We want to look more deeply at our data on sub-group populations in science…"*

*As district staff review data together with the school principal and site leadership team important academic patterns can be recognized. Collaborative data analysis also leads to creating a collaborative plan of action.

School Planning Conversations

Planning and goal setting is important for any successful organization. Planning is important for school organizations that want to make consistent improvement. Instructional planning should occur at the classroom level and at the same time it should occur at the school level. Principals and their leadership teams should make plans that will move the school organization forward.

School Planning Conversations Include:

- ❖ **Dialogue regarding standards and student's needs**
- ❖ **Clarifying of school goals and classroom objectives**
- ❖ **Establishing written goals and objectives**
- ❖ **Determining what the outcomes will look like**
- ❖ **Discussing how you will know when you have achieved the stated goals and objectives**

When we are transparent about the plans we make, we have a greater commitment to seeing these plans come to fruition. Let's take the opportunity to consider a sample school planning conversation between a district facilitator and school principal.

School Planning Example

District Facilitator: *"What plans and goals are you considering?"*

Chief Contributor/Principal: *"Well as we have looked over the data and talked with teachers, the admin team believes that we need continue to focus on. We are concerned about*

District Facilitator: *"How do the district's initiatives fit in with school plans?"*

Chief Contributor/Principal: *"Well the initiative on differentiated instruction is definitely making an impact and we are seeing results."*

District Facilitator: *"What seems to be working particularly well with your efforts in differentiated instruction?"*

Chief Contributor/Principal: *"We are seeing many of our students that are close to meeting proficiency standards more easily achieve their growth targets.*

District Facilitator: *"Great, We look forward to hearing about improved results as students continue to receive differentiated instruction."*

*The plans that schools make will create a collective commitment from the members of the school leadership team, and it will enlist the support of district staff responsible for improving instructional results.

Creating School Solutions Conversations

The creating solutions portion of the academic conference is optional. The district facilitator should check with the chief contributor or principal to see if they would like to take the time to address a specific area of need. While some principals may want to brainstorm and discuss potential solutions, others may feel that they have a clear idea about how to move the school organization forward.

School Solutions Conversations Include:

* ❖ **Dialogue regarding standards and student's needs**
* ❖ **Clarifying of school goals and classroom objectives**
* ❖ **Establishing written goals and objectives**
* ❖ **Determining what the outcomes will look like**
* ❖ **Discussing how you will know when you have achieved the stated goals and objectives**

Let's consider an example of creating a possible solution for an alternative high school.

Creating School Solutions Example

District Facilitator: *"As we look to continue the progress that has been made the past several months, where do you believe we need to create additional solutions?"*

Chief Contributor/Principal Alternative HS: *"We are pleased that we are seeing progress in attendance, yet teachers are reporting that many of our students are not completing reading assignments in class or finishing homework.*

District Facilitator: *"What do you think is the root cause of this issue, and what have you considered as a course of action?"*

Chief Contributor/Principal Alternative HS: *"We are unsure why we are hearing that reading and homework assignments are not being completed at an increasing rate. We have talked about it with the teachers and as an admin team and it is a big challenge."*

District Facilitator: "What did you come up with so far?"

Chief Contributor/Assistant Principal Alternative HS: "As we met with each other in our admin meeting, we thought about tutoring after school, yet we typically don't get very good attendance."

Principal Alternative HS: "We are really struggling, and could use some additional ideas."

District Facilitator: "Well let's see if we can consider a few options. District support team, what do you think we can do to help with this challenge?"

District Director of Instruction: "I have seen the emphasis on explicitly teaching text structure and signal words make a difference at Edison Middle School.

Director of Language Development: "Front-loading vocabulary has made a difference for students at Tukwila Elementary."

Principal: "The teachers have been mentioning that they want to do more with vocabulary instruction. That may be a good place for us to start."

District Facilitator: "That sounds great. Let's have the directors put together a staff training for your teachers that focuses on improving vocabulary instruction."

Principal: "Terrific. Let's schedule something on our first Tuesday of next month's staff development session."

District Facilitator: "Great. I am glad that we can be of some help."

* Conferral members only take the time to engage in the creating solutions process if there is a need to dig deep into a needed solution.

Making School Commitment Conversations

The school-administrator academic conference should conclude with a making commitment conversation. The principal and leadership team as the chief contributors should identify a specific area for school growth. The district leadership should make one commitment that they will provide to support the school leadership team to meet the area for school growth. The conference session should wrap up with the school leadership team making three commitments from the plans that they outlined previously in the planning conversation. These three commitments should be written down as "We will ..." statements.

School Commitment Conversations Include:

❖ **Dialogue regarding standards and student's needs**
❖ **Clarifying of school goals and classroom objectives**
❖ **Establishing written goals and objectives**
❖ **Determining what the outcomes will look like**
❖ **Discussing how you will know when you have achieved the stated goals and objectives**

Now we can look at an example of making and confirming commitments for an elementary principal.

Making Commitments Example

District Facilitator: "What are the three commitments you and your team will be focusing your energy for the next three months?"

Chief Contributor/K-8 Principal: "As an admin team, we have given this a lot of thought. We want to continue to focus on ELL's so we are targeting a goal of making sure another 30% of our intermediate ELL"s progress to the next level of early advanced. We want to improve our reading scores in grades 3-6, so we are initiating a deployment model of reading intervention. We want to increase our 7-8 math scores and better prepare our students for algebra, so we will bring in a trainer for all of our teachers in these two grades."

District Facilitator: *"What do the commitments look like as far outcomes?"*

Chief Contributor/K-8 Principal: *"One, we will move 30% of our intermediate ELL's to early advanced by the end of the school year. Two, we will initiate a 40 minute daily session of deployment to target student's reading scores in grades 3-5. Three, we will provide training for our 6- 8 grade teachers which we believe will better prepare our students for algebra."*

District Facilitator: *"How do your teachers feel about these three commitments?"*

Chief Contributor/K-8 Principal: *"Our teachers have expressed a concern about the number of ELL's who are struggling to progress and they are excited to deploy students and target in on specific reading strategies for different groups. Our 6-8 grade teachers are looking forward to getting training in Algebra principles and they helped pick out the training program."*

District Facilitator: *"We look forward to hearing how things go with these commitments."*

District Facilitator: *"So as you consider the things you have learned, what are some commitments that you and the school administrative team believe will make a difference for your students?"*

Chief Contributor/Principal: *"As we looked at the data, we definitely see a need to continue working with our English Language Learners, and we will*

District Facilitator: *"What else*

Chief Contributor/Principal: *"We want to continue*

District Facilitator: *"What can the district do to support your school?*

Chief Contributor/Principal: *"We appreciate the support*

*The making commitment conversation that concludes the conferral session gives the academic conference a defined direction for the collective efforts of everyone involved. Commitments provide a clear focus for the school leadership team as the move forward. These school commitments should be taken back to the school staff and teachers so that everyone at the school can focus on accomplishing these outcomes.

It should be noted that it may take an entire year of conferences to cycle through each phase of the feedback spiral, and that they do not necessarily occur in a specific order. At the end of the year, the professional stakeholders will have a clear plan and understanding of student data and have solutions and ongoing commitments that will sustain academic success.

Asking the Focus Question?

One of the key elements for coordinating an effective academic conference is the quality of questions that the district leadership asks of the school principal and site leadership team. Questions that are effectively presented to principals will engage principals in thinking that will provide creative solutions to the challenges our students face. Academic conferences create the context where a shift in the conversation can focus on instructional processes. Consider a few examples of questions to focus conferral conversations.

- *"What can we do to improve results for our English Language Learners?"*

- *"What types of interventions are working and what else can we do to reach struggling students?"*

- *"What can we do to structure our Professional Learning Communities (PLC's) so that they are even more effective?"*

- *"What are you seeing in your observational walks through classrooms?"*

- *"How is our current professional development being implemented in the classroom, and what professional development will help your staff going forward.*

The key to the effective questions is to improve the thinking and self-directed learning capacity of principals and the school's leadership team. Building the capacity to think positively, strategically, and creatively is a talent that our schools need to nurture among its administrative leaders, classroom leaders, and student leaders. Great leaders can communicate effectively through healthy dialogue, and they make good decisions through group discussion. We all want to part of the dialogue regarding the matters that affect us and we want to be part of the discussion regarding the decisions that will be made. Participating in the dialogue and discussion includes us in the understanding and decision making processes that ultimately are implemented at school sites in our classrooms.

School Leadership Pool of Assets

While school-administrator conferences provide tremendous benefits to the entire school organization, the benefits to the individual members of the site leadership team are also significant. The conferral process helps bring a higher level of thinking and metacognitive reflection of administrators to the surface. The individual experience and expertise of site administrators is valued. Creativity is encouraged. The site administrators can share their knowledge of teachers and their individual and collective strengths with district leaders. Teamwork skills are emphasized and developed, while the leadership capacity of school administrators are given an opportunity to flourish. Land & Jarman (1992) note that,

> *"Teamwork is the ability to work together toward a common vision — the ability to direct individual accomplishment toward organizational objectives. [Teamwork] is the fuel that allows common people to accomplish uncommon results."*

A primary purpose of school-administrator conferences is to develop the capacity and skills of the entire district organization. At the same time these conferral sessions are designed to increase the individual capacity of all administrators.

School-Administrator Academic Conference Form

Chief Contributor	Mr. Carney – School Principal and Team	Date	October 13th
Facilitator	Dr. Drummond – Assistant Superintendent of Instruction		
Participants	Dr. Marigold – District Superintendent, Mrs. Flanagan – Director of Special Ed, Dr. Esparza – Director of Language Development, Mr. Sanders – Director of Assessment		

❶ Reflecting:

Focus Question (Facilitator): "Which instructional initiatives are paying dividends for your school?"

Reflection (Chief Contributor): Key Points –We are seeing great success with improving academic language. Our ELL students are making the most progress. We are also seeing positive results with our after school tutoring program.

❺ Analyzing Data:

Analyze Data (Facilitator)
- School-wide English Benchmark Data &School-wide Mathematics Benchmark Data

Identify Five Student Groups: *(Chief Contributor)*

	Name	Target/Needs
1	English Language Learners	Make sure that teachers have three days of professional development training in SDAIE strategies.
2	Special Education Students	Increase the key academic language terms students know for their grade level.
3	Low Socio-Economic Students	Students need to increase their reading comprehension scores through inferencing skill development
4	RTI (Tier II) Students	Track the academic progress for all 24 Tier II students in the Response To Intervention initiative.
5	Kindergartners	Students need to count to 100 in math and be able to produce basic sounds and recognize all letters of the alphabet

❸ Planning: Set Three Goals *(Chief Contributor)*

1	**Commitment #1:** *We will observe at least 20 classrooms each week to ensure the instructional strategies covered in the recent professional collaboration session are effectively implemented.*
2	**Commitment #2:** *We will track English Language Learners benchmark scores in each grade and achieve a 10% increase in overall benchmark results for ELLs.*
3	**Commitment#3:** *We will reduce the number of students by 20% who are not reading at grade level .*

(OPTIONAL) Creating Solutions:

Creating Solutions (Chief Contributor): "Things seem to be going well so I don't have any major solutions for now."

Providing Suggestions *(Facilitator):* "Great to hear, let's now confirm our goals and commitments."

❶ Confirming Commitments

Identify One Professional Growth Area (Chief Contributor):
Growth Area: "We are focused on improving our intervention time every day from 1:30 to 2:10."

Make Commitment and Confirm Teacher Commitments (Facilitator):
Commitment support from the principal: "The district directors for special ed English Language Learners, assessment, and the assistant superintendent of instruction will stop by school intervention time once a week and provide feedback to staff.

Achieving Effective School-Administrator Conferences

Overall the school-administrator conference brings a principal, teacher, and site support staff and focuses them on a conferral process that is focused on student learning and improving instruction.

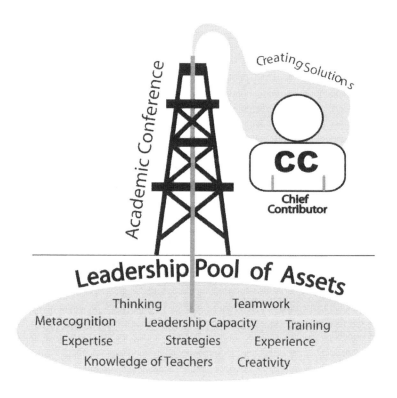

Figure 7.2: *School-Administrator Academic Conferences help tap into administrator's pool of leadership assets*

Over time, as the district and site leaders engage in the conferral process, a positive pool of leadership assets will develop and come to the surface in ways that benefit the entire district organization. The end result of school-administrator conferences is we will develop as professional and our students will also benefit academically. The benefit of this collegial environment is greater teamwork between school leaders and teacher leaders. We need to develop the leadership habits and skills of our school and district administrators. Academic conferences create the perfect venue for making sure that instructional leadership is not left to happenstance. School-administrator conferences ultimately develop the expertise, thinking, and teamwork of school principals and their leadership teams. Creating opportunities for their abilities to surface will strengthen the confidence of school leaders. The principal in their role as chief contributor of the school-administrator conference will find a wealth of resources that they recognize from within. While instructional leadership may be an innate quality for some, we all need opportunities to allow our best professional thinking to surface.

Summary

We need to do more than as educational teachers and leaders than to merely state our hopes and think about our dreams for our students. Instead, we should coordinate our resources and collaborate towards sustainable actions and consistent results. Through academic conferences, we can meet together and clearly outline our organizational and personal expectations and vision. After taking action, we can meet again and follow through on the progress towards the accomplishment of the vision. We need to continue to meet and reflect on our results and the lessons learned along the way. We must establish for each classroom a clear academic plan and successful academic practice while tracking the academic progress of every student. Teachers and leaders need to take a look back at their progress towards instructional expectations and look forward to outlining future instructional plans. Creating a stronger culture where student learning and instructional leadership are the norm provides for greater student learning. Our classrooms and schools face a variety of challenges. When our school's academic processes are coordinated and aligned, student learning can improve dramatically. Knowing how to engage in the dialogue of school-administrator academic conferences will help the overall district organization achieve success. Just as teachers need opportunities to share all that they do in the classroom, school administrators also benefit from opportunities to reflect on lessons by looking at data of their school's performance.

Reflection Questions

1. *How does your district develop instructional leadership throughout the organization from top to bottom?*

2. *How can academic conferences help your district get the right data and feedback to insure individuals within the organization are accountable for academic results?*

Chapter Eight:

Leading and Sustaining

Academic Conferences

"Learning organizations are organizations where people continually expand their capacity to create the results they truly desire, where new and expansive patterns of thinking are nurtured, where collective aspiration is set free, and where people are continually learning to see the whole together."

Peter Senge

Todd was excited to wrap-up the last conference of the year with Mr. Williams and the school's leadership team. As a first year science teacher he wanted to share so many things that his student's had achieved throughout the year and particularly in the past two months. Mr. Williams noticed that the dialogue was clearly focused on student learning results, and the discussion addressed ways to improve classroom instruction for kids. While Todd had struggled with achieving the commitments he made early in the year, a smile spread across his face because he had achieved his last three commitments made eight weeks earlier. He brought student writing to show their progress in identifying the investigation process. Mr. Williams could hardly wait for the next year to start. They had momentum.

Todd was so excited about his professional learning focus that he blurted out, "My kids are really responding to the strategies that I learned from the book you got me." It was a great year, and he was looking forward to next year and using all that he had learned right from the start.

Benefits of Classroom-Teacher Academic Conferences

Skillfully implemented academic conferences develop several core principles within teachers and administrators. Academic conferences are all about identifying successful practices, recognizing areas for learning, and finding areas where real support can be provided to enhance student progress. When teachers and leaders work together, then they can further develop their instructional leadership, internal locus of control, and self-directed learning. Ultimately this will lead to teachers and leaders better equipped to create sustainable solutions for all of our students. The Academic Conference is a time to share thinking, and engage in the best practices to execute for the situation at hand.

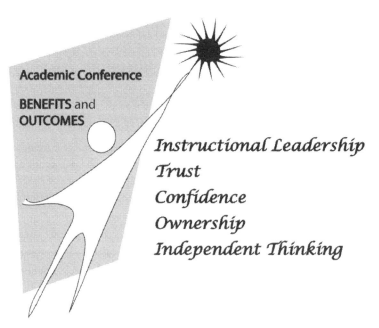

Figure 8.1: Major benefits and outcomes of effectively run academic conferences

If we are going to construct a high quality learning organization, then we need to capture the high quality thinking available within the organization. Academic conferences when executed effectively create several major organizational benefits:

Key Outcomes Achieved by Academic Conferences

- ❖ **Developing Instructional Leadership**
- ❖ **Creating Trust & Confidence**
- ❖ **Taking Ownership**
- ❖ **Developing Independent Learning**

Over time the benefits of academic conferences will create a stronger learning organization and culture of success.

Instructional Leadership

Part of what the academic conference is made to do is strengthen relationships between the faculty and school administrators. Often teachers and administrators find themselves with strained relationships. People don't feel like they are on the same team. When both commit to being instructional leaders, everyone is on the same team. The focus is on instructional leadership: working together to creating solutions for students. McCauley et al. (2008)

> *"Interdependent leadership cultures and practices are broadly characterized by the assumption that leadership is a collective activity that requires mutual inquiry and learning. Other characteristics associated with interdependent cultures include the following: the ability to work effectively across organizational boundaries, openness and candor, multifaceted standards of success, and synergies being sought across the whole enterprise."*

These academic conferences must occur regularly throughout the school year. They initiate processes that are capable of transforming individuals each and every day, and thus they must happen on a consistent basis. Relationships are only built through consistency. Academic conferences are much more than just an ad hoc meeting thrown together throughout the school year. The sessions embrace a variety of focused processes that spiral through and transform the thinking and actions of the most important individuals in the success of our students—teachers, principals, and district administrators. The point of these conferences is to provide a place and time for the academic leaders of the school to have focused conversations that create real results

Taking Ownership

Academic conferences support a school culture that emphasizes internal accountability. This internal accountability may more appropriately be called ownership. Honoring the voices and choices of the chief contributors, encourages the development of each individual's internal locus of control. They take ownership of the issues students bring with them. They look at the issues that face their students and choose to actively take the time to consider creative solutions to their challenges. They insist that those students leave their classroom better than when they came in that day. *This* is ownership. If we are to have this resolve to improve in every part of our schools, we can collectively do so much more. To improve our profession Price Waterhouse Coopers (2001) again point out that,

> *"An essential strand will be to reduce teacher workload, foster increased teacher ownership, and create the capacity to manage change in a sustainable way that can lay the foundation for improved school and pupil performance in the future."*

Providing support that teachers declare will make a difference will help reduce their workload and increase productivity. Making specific commitments to take action towards progress in student learning is essential to the success of our students. We need to empower people to take ownership for their actions and their results. Traditional approaches to school accountability create compliance without commitment and emphasize involvement without real investment. On the other hand, creating a culture of ownership through academic conferences produces long-lasting commitment and an internal investment in students and their learning.

Self-Directed Learning

At the core of student learning and quality instruction is a classroom that develops self-directed learning. The ultimate purpose of the classroom-teacher academic conference is for teachers to become more self-directed learners. Teachers become more self-directed learners as they develop a greater internal locus of control and embrace greater instructional leadership. Schein (2004) notes the importance of leaders working with individual:

> *"It is essential to involve learners in designing their own optimal learning process."*

The classroom-teaching academic conference provides a forum for building a foundation of self-directed learning that leads to life-long learning for teachers. The school-administrator academic conferences do the same thing for school principals. Self-Directed Learning is a communication and thought process that invites individuals to take control of their own learning. As educators enhance self-directed learning, they better understand their own internal processes that shape personal growth. Academic conferences focus on classroom success and place the teacher at the center of the classroom learning equation and principals at the center of the school learning equation. Working together in academic conference provides a forum for educators to connect their own vision, values, and voice with their colleagues. These conferences turn our good ideas and intentions into proven relationships and results. Teachers will take ownership of learning and instruction because the structure of the conference sessions makes these processes explicit. Teachers who fully develop their abilities as self-directed learners take ownership of the learning process. They embrace learning within their students, within themselves, and within the school organization. Conferring encourages a safe environment where experimentation encourages an atmosphere of choice, risk-taking and inquiry exists. Data is analyzed without concern that they will be used as a basis for evaluating success or failure. Creativity will more likely grow in a supportive atmosphere.

Generating Confidence & Trust

The school leadership team develops greater confidence as they tackle the real issues that will improve student learning and instruction. Confidence comes from our individual ability to meet challenges and come up with actions that will produce results. Academic conferences develop the individual confidence of teachers as they help increase their ability to reflect, analyze data, plan, create solutions, and make commitments. Lykins (2012) points out that confidence grows as instructional leaders align, plan, and work together to create results.

Academic Alignment makes sure that school-wide efforts the professional development, the Response to Intervention, the Professional Learning Communities, the analysis of student data, and the observations of student learning contribute to student learning for all groups of students. It also means alignment with the classroom efforts of standards-based objectives, lesson design, instructional practice, intervention strategies, and student engagement contribute to individual learning for every student.

Academic Plans so often it seems that it is just make it through another semester or year. When do we ever talk about what we are going to do for groups of students who are struggling? When do we ever talk about the students who are being left behind in their learning? We need to be explicit about our goals for these students and clearly outline and plan the steps that it will take to ensure they achieve these learning goals. The key window of time according to research on instructional interventions is three to Six month. We need to accelerate student learning so that they can catch up to grade level peers.

Academic Collegiality When the learning becomes interdependent. When we realize that we are all in this together. When scholarship and sharing of our best ideas, best practices, and best efforts. We know that support

Academic Results zeroing in on student achievement for every student. It is important that we extinguish the achievement gaps within our classrooms and our schools.

Academic conferences help with the alignment, goals, collegiality, and results of the school organization. This process benefits as everyone embraces trust, and in fact the process actually builds trust. Through the conferencing process, teachers learn to trust the instructional focus of administrators and administrators learn to trust and support the instructional decisions of the teachers. This mutual trust and respect rewards both teachers and administrators, while the students become the ultimate beneficiaries Sutton and Wheatley (2003) outline three areas that support the development of trust:

Developing Trust

  ❖ *Share Important Information*
  ❖ *Build Caring Relationships*
  ❖ *Pursue Common Purposes*

Effective academic conferences build an atmosphere of trust with every teacher as important information is shared, relationships with students are discussed, and instructional purposes are shared and collectively pursued.

Implementation

Every year our schools have academic initiatives that they wish to implement for the benefit of students. Most initiatives rarely make the impact that they are designed to make. They achieve limited success to the point it is difficult to see if they had any impact at all on the bottom line—student learning. Schools need to align the vision and thinking as well as the values and feelings of everyone within the organization. District leaders need to work with school leaders, and in turn school leaders need to work with classroom leaders to achieve the collective vision of the entire organization. Academic conferences provide the forum for implementing the major initiatives agreed upon by district and site leaders.

Vertical Alignment through Academic Conferences

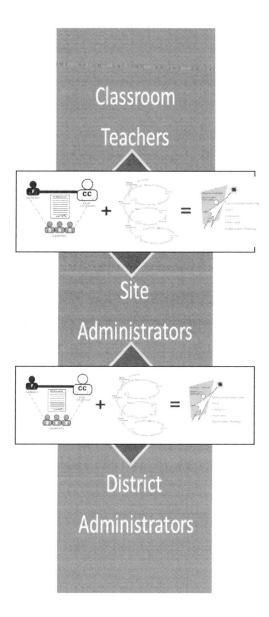

Figure 8.2: Effectively implemented academic conferences increase organizational capacity and sustainable results

Academic conferences connect teachers, site administrators, and district administrators vertically through dialogue that creates collegial relationships and interdependent leadership. Creating vertical alignment and interdependent relationships through academic conferences can fundamentally improve the way we work as professionals. Academic conferences link district administrators with site administrators and in turn with classroom teachers.

Capacity Building

The end result of academic conferences is that they develop individual leadership capacities amongst teacher and school leaders. The entire organization benefits when individuals within our schools are able to better develop their own improvement processes. Feuerstein & Falik (1981) note that,

> *"A goal of education, therefore, is to assist growth toward greater complexity and integration and to assist in the process of self-organization—to modify individuals' capacity to modify themselves."*

Through the processes of self-managing, self-monitoring and self-modifying, teachers are more able to fully embrace self-directed learning and develop a greater internal locus of control. They increase their ability to manage the instruction in their classroom, monitor their behavior and the behavior of their students, and modify it to improve their own instructional practice and student learning. While academic conferences do provide a forum for implementing academic initiatives, more importantly academic conferences are designed to build the individual capacity of everyone within our schools. As each individual develops their capacity, the collective capacity of the organization will also increase. Capacity building is all about bringing the talents of classroom leaders and school leaders to the table. Many a teachers talents go untapped. We have expertise, experience, and effective practice that rarely sees it to the light of day outside of individual classrooms. Just as academic conferences brought to light the discoveries of scientists and built their profession this past century, academic conferences can bring to light the talents of our current teacher leaders. It is important to state that every teacher can become a classroom leader with the right amount of support, care, and attention.

Sustainability

Sustainability takes time to develop. While many initiatives never really make it off the ground before they are left in the dust, and most schools are limit their ability to build the capacity of its members, creating real sustainability is the most difficult to achieve. Several years of effective implementation and capacity building are needed to show sustainable results. Sustainability must be consistent over time and include everyone associated with academic success. Coordinating academic conferences several times a year is a crucial step in creating sustainable results. Academic conferences create sustainable results, because they include every individual that is directly involved with academics throughout the entire school organization. Whether it is the district superintendent, district administrators, site principals, academic coaches, or classroom teachers, academic conferences are inclusive. They are places where everyone can dialogue openly about the important matters of academic progress and success. They also provide a forum for discussing those issues that can be improved. McCauley et al. (2008) notes the importance of collaborative trust,

> *"This collaborative work brings people with diverse perspectives together for mutual influence, co-construction of new perspectives, and self-authorized decision making (i.e., the decisions don't need to be approved at higher levels in the organization). The goal of the collaborative work is to maximize system effectiveness and learning."*

Building a stable environment where everyone's capabilities can positively impact the districts initiatives is a vital part of creating healthy schools. The academic conference specifically guides school and teacher leaders to achieve the following six principles for academic success.

Six Guiding Principles of Classroom-Teacher Academic Conference

1. Academic Conferences are designed to focus on student learning and quality instruction.
2. Academic Conferences begin with a Focus Question and encourage teacher reflection and open dialogue.
3. Academic Conferences look at student data and classroom experiences from which instructional insights can be made.
4. Academic Conferences provide time for reflecting, planning, and collaborating between instructional leaders.
5. Academic Conferences place administrators in the role of instructional facilitator and clear commitments.
6. Academic Conferences place students (and the teachers who know them best) at the center of the learning equation.

As we develop collegiality by consistently creating an open dialogue about the important issues of school, then we will achieve greater teamwork, trust, and results. The essence of building trust and collegiality is to better understand how to work together as a unit. People are more likely to engage and grow in higher-level, creative, and experimental thought when they are in a trusting, risk-taking, and cooperative climate.

> . . . *Albert, Marie, and Ernest wrote to one another and compared notes after the academic conference and continued their collegial dialogue that both challenged and elevated their own thinking. They looked forward to getting back to their research and continuing anew their professional pursuits to further their understanding of scientific principles. They each anticipated the time when they would be able to reconvene at the next academic conference and engage in more collegial conversations that would improve their practice and profession.*

Summary

As the school district leaders facilitate a conferral discussion with school administrators,   While just taking the time to sit down together and dialogue openly about school progress is beneficial, coordinating a conference session that is purposefully crafted can create benefits in instructional leadership, trust and confidence, educational ownership, and independent thinking. The unity and trust that develops will pay dividends for many years to come. Academic conferences provide a forum for teachers and leaders to make sure that our students do not slip through the cracks, gaps, and chasms. They support a school culture of self-directed learning and collegial cooperation in behalf of students and the challenges they face. The conferences develop true ownership or internal accountability for the actions that teachers and administrators take towards instruction. Effective conferencing creates greater understanding throughout the organization. They increase instructional leadership, create greater trust and confidence, encourage ownership, and develop the independent thinking of school administrators. Through periodic conferencing district administrators have a clearer idea of what is happening at the school level, and they receive insights into academic progress and are better able to identify areas that need support. School administrator conferences achieve results because of the quantitative data and the qualitative dialogue helps determine how individual schools are doing and how the overall district is performing. Effective school administrator conferences conducted across the district have the power to elevate the results of each school and each classroom.

Reflection Questions

1. *How does your district develop instructional leadership throughout the organization from top to bottom?*

2. *How can academic conferences help your district get the right data and feedback to insure individuals within the organization are accountable for academic results?*

Appendix A:
Certification for Academic Conference

School district organizations that would like to fully implement academic conference in their schools are eligible for Academic Conference Certification. The certification process is a structured method for improving classrooms and school throughout an entire district. School districts may begin the official process for certification by engaging in the following steps.

The purpose of certification is to…

❖ Ensure implementation of a high-quality School-wide Academic Conference program.

❖ Support capacity building of individuals within the school organization.

❖ Create a sustainable system for ensuring continued academic success at the school.

❖ Recognize schools that are committed to supporting self-directed learning and academic leadership.

The Four-step certification process involves…

1. Initial school-wide training

2. Academic Conference visits and feedback

3. Second year follow-up training

4. Final certification report

Full implementation of the academic training certification is typically a two year process for implementation. If you are implementing Academic Conferences at your school and are interested in certified recognition, please contact certification@academicconferences.org .

Benefits for Schools

❖ Students and parents know that they are attending a school that has cohesive classroom and a school leadership.

❖ Teachers may be certified as approved for academic conferencing classroom excellence award.

❖ Principals and Site Leaders may be certified as approved for academic conferencing school excellence award.

❖ Greater visibility for the school program within the school and community.

Four Steps to a School's Classroom-Teacher Certification

Step 1: Initial School-wide training:

❖ Schedule five day academic conference training for all site administrators, teachers, and academic support staff.

❖ Partnership schools are established to provide support for the program and site and classroom leaders.

❖ The academic conference trainings are taught by administrators and teachers who have received the Academic Conference Advanced Training certification.

Step 2: Academic Conference visits and feedback

❖ Complete the *Academic Conference Self-Assessment* and submit to at least two months prior to the desired site visit date.

❖ An implementation and capacity building plan are in place for the program.

❖ Coordinate two days of Academic Conference visits later in the initial school year where processes can be modeled and observed by trainer.

Step 3: Second year follow-up training

❖ Schedule three day Academic Conference follow-up training for all site administrators, teachers, and academic staff.

❖ Facilitators demonstrate mastery of questioning, listening, dialogue, discussion, and conferral protocols for the trainer and a majority of teachers demonstrate mastery of self-directed learning skills.

❖ Trainer confirms that Academic Conferences continue to be implemented effectively.

Step 4: Final Certification Report

❖ Complete the final Academic Conference Self-Assessment
❖ Receive approval from your trainer and Academic Conference site visitor.
❖ Complete the Academic Conference plan to outline continued capacity and sustainability results.
❖ Receive final certification to display to your parents, school board, and community.

Certification for District's School-Administrator Academic Conference

In addition to the Certification for schools, District Certification for School-Administrator Academic Conferences is also available. Districts will need to have a team of district educators trained at advanced training session and conduct consistent training sessions for their districts. Outside trainers will need to make visits to the district and school sites to authorize the certification process. To learn more about the District-wide certification please contact certification@academicconferences.org.

However you implement academic conferences, we wish you the best in your pursuit of improved instruction and increased student learning through your school organization. Thanks for all that you do for kids and for your colleagues.

Academic Conferences References

Christensen, C. (2012) The Innovator's Dilemma: When new Technologies cause great firms to fail with award winning Harvard Business Review articles. Boston, MA: Harvard Business Press.

Cohen, D. & Prusak, L. (2001) In Good Company: How social capital makes organizations work. Boston, MA: Harvard Business School.

Collins, J. (2001) Good to Great: Why some companies make the leap … and others don't. New York, NY: Harper-Collins.

Costa, A. & Garmston, R. (2002) Cognitive Coaching: A foundation for Renaissance Schools. Norwood, MA: Christopher Gordon Publishers

Costa, A. & Kallick, B. (2003) Assessment Strategies for Self-Directed Learners: Thousand Oaks, CA: Corwin Press.

Costa, A. (2007) The School as a Home of the Mind: Creating mindful curriculum, instruction, and dialogue. Thousand Oaks, CA: Corwin Press.

Deming, E. (2000) The New Economic for Business, Government, and Education. Boston, MA: MIT Press.

DuFour, R., DuFour, R., Eaker, R., & Many, T. (2010) Learning by Doing. Bloomington, IN: Solution Tree Press

DuFour, R., & Marzano, R. J. (2011) Leaders of learning: How district, school, and classroom leaders improve student achievement. Bloomington, IN: Solution Tree Press.

Feuerstein, R. & Falik, L. (2010) Beyond Smarter: Mediated learning and brain's capacity for change. New York, NY: Teacher College Press.

Fullan, M. (2002) The Change Leader. Educational Leadership. 59 (3) 14-20.

Fullan, M. (1993). Change forces: Probing the depths of educational reform (Vol. 10). Routledge.

Frymier, J. (1987) Bureaucracy and the neutering of teachers. Phi Delta Kappan 69-1 9-14.

Garmston, R. (2005) Interview conducted on September 26, 2005. Found at http://www.adaptiveschools.com/ednewsinterviewrgarmston.htm

Garmston, R. & Wellman, R. (2008) The Adaptive School: A sourcebook for developing collaborative groups. (2nd Ed.) Norwood, MA: Christopher Gordon Publishers.

Hargreaves, A. (1998) The Emotional Practice of Teaching. Teaching and Teacher Education (14) 8 p. 835-854.

Harris, A. & Lambert, L. (2003) Building Leadership Capacity for School. Berkshire England: Open University Press.

Jarvis, M. (2003) "Teacher stress." A Critical Review of Recent Finding and Suggestions for Future Research Direction. Stress News. Retrieved March 10 (2003): 33-60.

Johnson, E. & Karns, M. (2011) RTI Strategies that work in the 3-6 classroom. Larchmont, NY: Eye on Education.

Johnson, E. (2012). Academic Language & Academic Vocabulary: A K-12 Guide to content learning and RTI. Sacramento, CA: Achievement For All Publishers.

Leithwood, K. & Poplin , M. (1992) The move towards transformational leadership. Educational Leadership. (49) 5 p. 8.

Lipton, L. & Wellman, B. (2000) Pathways to understanding: Patterns and practices in the learning-focused classroom. Sherman, CT: MiraVia, LLC.

Lipton, L. & Wellman, B. (2001) Mentoring Matters: A practical guide to learning-focused relationships. Sherman, CT: MiraVia, LLC.

Louis, K., Marks, H., & Kruse, S. (1996) Teacher's Professional Community in Restructuring Schools. American Educational Research Journal. 33(4) 757-798

Lykins, L. (2012) Getting Results: Aligning learning's goals with business performance. TD Magazine. April (9) p. 1-2.

Marzano, R. (2003) Using Data: Two wrongs and a right. Educational Leadership 60(5) 56-60.

Marzano, R., Pickering, D. & Pollock, J. (2001) Classroom Instruction that Works: Research-Based Strategies for increasing student achievement. Alexandria, VA: ASCD.

McCauley, C., Palus, C., Drath, W., Hughes, R., McGuire, J., O'Connor, P., & Van Velsor, E. (2008). Interdependent Leadership in Organizations: Evidence from six case studies. A Center for Creative Leadership Report.

Price Waterhouse Coopers (2001). Teacher Workload Study. London: Department for Education and Skills.

Rock, D. (2010). Your Brain at Work: Strategies for overcoming distraction, regaining focus, and working smarter all day long. New York, NY: Harper Business.

Sarason, S. (1990) The Predictable Failure of Educational Reform. San Francisco, CA: Jossey-Bass.

Schein, E. (2004) Organizational Culture and Leadership (3rd Edition). San Francisco, CA: Jossey-Bass.

Schon, D. (1983) The Reflective Practitioner. New York, NY: Basic Books.

Senge, P., Cambron-McCabe, N., Lucas, T. & Kleiner, A. (2000) Schools that Learn: A fifth discipline fieldbook for educators, parents, and everyone who cares about education. New York, NY: Crown Publishing.

Sutton, R. E., & Wheatley, K. F. (2003). Teachers' emotions and teaching: A review of the literature and directions for future research. Educational Psychology Review, 15, 327–358.

Zmuda, A. (2010) Breaking Free from Myths and Teaching and Learning: Innovation as an engine for student success. Alexandria, VA: ASCD

17527070R00081